MURDER

on the

ABARENDA

Marvin W. Barrash

HERITAGE BOOKS
2016

HERITAGE BOOKS
AN IMPRINT OF HERITAGE BOOKS, INC.

Books, CDs, and more—Worldwide

For our listing of thousands of titles see our website at
www.HeritageBooks.com

Published 2016 by
HERITAGE BOOKS, INC.
Publishing Division
5810 Ruatan Street
Berwyn Heights, Md. 20740

Copyright © 2016 Marvin W. Barrash

Heritage Books by the author:
Murder on the Abarenda
U.S.S. Cyclops

All rights reserved. No part of this book may be reproduced or transmitted in any form or by any means, electronic or mechanical, including photocopying, recording or by any information storage and retrieval system without written permission from the author, except for the inclusion of brief quotations in a review.

International Standard Book Numbers
Paperbound: 978-0-7884-5729-6
Clothbound: 978-0-7884-6473-7

For my wife Rebecca and my son Kyle

Dedicated to the Men of the *Abarenda*

Table of Contents

Preface vii

Acknowledgements ix

Robert and Viola Weichert 1
    Weichert - Patterson Wedding 2
    St. John the Baptist Church 3
    Children 4

Walter Robert Weichert's Sea Service 6
    Abarenda's First Officer 9
        Testimony of Harry M. Bostwick, third officer, U.S.A.S. Abarenda 15
        Testimony of William Easton, seaman, U.S.A.S. Abarenda. 16
    Official Report of Death 21

The District Court of the United States for Porto Rico 28
    Bernard S. Rodey, Judge 28
    José R.F. Savage, United States Attorney 29

Carpenter Dickson's Trial 31
    Chronology 31
    Statement to the Petit Jury by Bernard S. Rodey, Judge 33
    Instructions to the Petit Jury by Bernard S. Rodey, Judge 34
    Verdict 40
    Cause for an Additional Trial 41

Master Worley's Trial 42
    Complaint by Seaman Louis E. Chinal 44

Complaint by Seaman Patrick Gallagher 45
Complaint by Seaman George Marsden 45
Irons 54
Weichert in the Spanish American War 58
Widow's Pension 62
The Weichert Family Without Walter 93
Chief Officer Walter Robert Weichert's Final Rest 96
More Tragedies in the Life of Viola Weichert 98
    Mother Passed On 98
    Death of Father 99
    Homer Bird on Trial 104
        Justice 111
A History of the U.S.S. *Abarenda* 112
    Born in England 112
    Freighter *Abarenda* 115
    Collier *Abarenda* 117
    Freighter *Antonio*, then Scrap 122
    Abarenda's Scrap Paper 122
Index 125

Preface

"*'Tis strange - but true; for truth is always strange, Stranger than fiction...*"[1] The events that follow, fit that statement well. For it would be quite difficult to craft such a tragic tale, so detrimental to a family.

As the title indicates, the initial focus of this volume concerns the heinous murder that took place on board the United States collier *Abarenda* in 1908. It will soon come to light that the brutal death of the ship's second in command was but one of a series of terrible tragedies that befell a family. In their day, each of those incidences quickly became sensationalized stories in newspapers across the country. With the passage of time, those events slipped into obscurity - until now. On the surface it may appear that this is a *whodunit* mystery story, in fact, it is anything but that.

The timeframe for this book may be quite unfamiliar to many. While modern technology, such as the telephone and telegraph existed back then, not everyone had access to it. Instantaneous communication was not there for all. During the timeframe of this narrative, one could send the written word across the United States for a couple of cents. Several days later it would arrive by letter carrier at its destination. With patience, a reply would eventually be received.

The *Abarenda* was not a famous passenger ship or a glorious battleship. She was just a typical ocean-going vessel, built on the River Tyne, for international trade. After several years, she was sold to another nation and refitted for naval service. She would eventually return to commercial shipping with a new name and once again, under a different flag.

---

[1] Don Juan, Canto XIV, St. 91-101, *The Works of Lord Byron Complete in One Volume*, Francfort O.M., Printed by and for H.L. Brœnner, 1826, p. 316

I previously wrote about the U.S.S. *Cyclops*[2]. Through that research I first learned that the ship's captain, George W. Worley had previously commanded the collier *Abarenda* during some of her darkest days in which one of his senior officers was murdered. Were that not enough, the captain himself faced serious charges concerning his own conduct. That was the basis for my investigation of the *Murder on the Abarenda*. Not anticipating it, the timeframe of my research needed to expand by decades. I was more than pleased at the amount of documentation that survived the years that could help to unravel the manifold events herein.

The author sincerely acknowledges the great assistance provided to him by the many librarians, archivists and staff who made available the source documentation for this book. My heartfelt thanks to Ms. Lucille Weichert Croscup, granddaughter of Walter R. Weichert for her gracious insight concerning her family.

Marvin William Barrash
June 12, 2016

---

[2] U.S.S. CYCLOPS, Heritage Books, 2010

Acknowledgements

Beth Adams

Freya Anderson, Head, Information Services,
    Alaska State Library, Juneau, AK

Patricia Behles,
    University of Baltimore Law Library, Baltimore, MD

Germain J. Bienvenu, Special Collections Public Services,
    Louisiana State University Libraries

Matthew E. Braun, Legal Reference Librarian,
    The Law Library of Congress, Washington, DC

Todd Creekman (CAPT, USN Ret.), Executive Director, Naval
    Historical Foundation

Joanne Dugan Colvin, Assoc. Dir. for Public Services,
    University of Baltimore Law Library, Baltimore, MD

Paula Cosner

Lucille W. Croscup,
    Granddaughter of Walter Robert Weichert

Dorenda Dupont, Archives Staff, Office of Archives and Records,
    Archdiocese of New Orleans, Louisiana

Linda Edwards, Navy Department Library,
    Washington Navy Yard, Washington, DC

Davis Elliott, Navy Department Library,
    Washington Navy Yard, Washington, DC

Mark L. Evans, Historian, Naval History & Heritage Command,
    Washington Navy Yard, Washington, DC

Tina Hampson

Robert Hanshew - Photo Curator,
	Naval History & Heritage Command,
	Washington Navy Yard, Washington, DC

David A. Hatch

Glenn Helm, Director,
	Navy Department Library,
	Washington Navy Yard, Washington, DC

Chris Killilay,
	National Archives and Records Administration,
	Washington, DC

James A. Knechtmann, Navy Department Library,
	Washington Navy Yard, Washington, DC

Karen Needles, Director,
	Lincoln Archives Digital Project

Young Park, Navy Department Library,
	Washington Navy Yard, Washington, DC

Vincent J. Patterson

Greg Plunges, Archivist,
	National Archives and Records Administration,
	New York, NY

Stephen S. Roberts, ShipScribe.com

Dennis Riley, National Archives and Records Administration,
	New York, NY

Rod Ross, Center for Legislative Archives,
> National Archives and Records Administration,
> Washington, DC

Bonnie M. Sauer - National Archives and Records Administration,
> New York, NY

Tonya Simpson, Navy Department Library,
> Washington Navy Yard, Washington, DC

Rene Stein, Librarian,
> National Cryptologic Museum, Annapolis Junction, MD

Tatyana Stepanova, Archivist,
> Alaska State Archives, Juneau, AK

Trina Yeckley, National Archives and Records Administration,
> New York, NY

*"... Carpenter killed Walter Weichert, Chief Officer, Abarenda today.³
Rohrer"⁴*

---

³ Commodore, Karl Rohrer (retired), Commandant, Naval Station, San Juan, PR to Bureau of Navigation, Washington, D.C., February 20, 1908; p. 344, San Juan Naval Station Cablegrams, Entry 739, Records of Naval Station San Juan, P.R., Naval Districts and Shore Establishments, Record Group 181; National Archives and Records Administration - Northeast Region, New York City

⁴ *Register of the Commissioned and Warrant Officers of the United States Navy and Marine Corps*, Navy Department, U.S. Government Printing Office, Washington, DC, January 1, 1908, pp. 148, 225

Robert and Viola Weichert

Walter Robert Weichert was born on May 20, 1873[5] in New York City, N.Y.[6] A Department of the Navy file stated that his birth year was 1874.[7] The City of Boston's Birth Registry for 1904 and 1906, which listed two of his children, indicated that his place of birth was Switzerland. Walter Weichert was the son of Joseph W. Weichert and Mary Ludwig[8] and was the younger brother of Martha Klee who was born two years[9] earlier in Germany.[10] His other sisters were Marie Kaiser[11] and a Mrs. Cramer.[12]

Viola Ruth Patterson was born on August 25, 1878 in New Orleans, Louisiana. Her parents were Robert L. Patterson, age 23 and Katie Healy, age 22. Both of her parents were born in

---

[5] Record of Interment, Department of the Army Form 2122, Veterans Administration, Washington, DC

[6] Enlistment record, Walter R. Weichert, Albany, New York; Abstracts of Spanish-American War Military and Naval Service Records, 1898-1902; Series Number: B0809.

[7] 6th Endorsement, Subject: Bureau of Pensions: Requests descriptive list and history of service and circumstances surrounding the murder of Walter R. Weichert, Chief Officer, killed February 20, 1908, at San Juan, P.R., March 30, 1908, Edward B. Barry, Captain, U.S. Navy, Supervisor of Naval Auxiliaries, Department of the Navy information to be provided to Bureau of Pensions concerning Walter R. Weichert., Pension file no. 925721, Walter R. Weichert, Record Group 15, National Archives Building, Washington, DC

[8] Record of Marriage, Weichert/Patterson, State of Louisiana, Secretary of State, Division of Archives, Records Management, and History, Baton Rouge, LA

[9] Deposition, Martha Klee sworn before John F. Keeley, Notary Public, New York County, NY, November 18, 1922, Pension file no. 925721, Walter R. Weichert, Record Group 15, National Archives Building, Washington, DC

[10] 1910; Census, Manhattan Ward 16, New York, NY; Roll: T624_1035; p. 5B; Enumeration District: 0865; Image: 530; Records of the Bureau of the Census, Record Group 29, National Archives, Washington, DC

[11] Weichart [sic] Wedded Here, *The Daily Picayune*, New Orleans, LA, March 8, 1908, p. 4

[12] Mrs. Cramer resided at 99 Wales Avenue, Jersey City, NJ, Correspondence, 4th Endorsement, from W.R. Shoemaker, Commander, U.S. Navy to the Commissioner of Pensions, October 10, 1908, Pension file no. 925721, Record Group 15; National Archives Bldg., Washington, DC

New Orleans.[13]

Weichert - Patterson Wedding

The wedding of Mr. Walter R. Weichert of New York to Viola R. Patterson of New Orleans was described as "very pretty."[14] It was solemnized on April 21, 1903[15] at 8:00 p.m. at St. John the Baptist Church, on Dryades Street, New Orleans, Louisiana. Reverend Father James P. Malone officiated.[16]

In the Marriage Register was recorded, "On this 21st day of April 1903, I the undersigned having seen the license and having obtained a dispensation of *"Mixtae Religionis"*, have joined in the holy Bonds of Matrimony - Walter Robert Weichert - Son of Joseph W Weichert & Mary Ludwig - and Miss Viola Patterson - Daughter of Robert L. Patterson & Katie Healy." Signed by [Reverend Father] James P. Malone, W.R. Weichert, Viola Patterson. Also signed by: Marshall Casse, Cella Barr, John Hartings, John Van Names.[17]

The dispensation of *"Mixtae Religionis"* provided a formal authorization by the Church to proceed with the marriage of the Catholic bride to the non-Catholic groom. It may have required the signing of a promise by the groom not to interfere, "by word or act," with the bride's faith; not to prevent their

---

[13] Record of Marriage, Weichert/Patterson, State of Louisiana, Secretary of State, Division of Archives, Records Management, and History, Baton Rouge, LA
[14] WITCHERT [sic] – PATTERSON, *The Daily Picayune*, New Orleans, LA April 26, 1903, p. 11
[15] Record of Marriage, Weichert/Patterson, State of Louisiana, Secretary of State, Division of Archives, Records Management, and History, Baton Rouge, LA
[16] Record of Marriage, Weichert/Patterson, State of Louisiana, Secretary of State, Division of Archives, Records Management, and History, Baton Rouge, LA
[17] Marriage Register of St. John the Baptist Church, New Orleans, LA, Volume 5, 1900-1918, p. 75. Archives of the Archdiocese of New Orleans

child[ren] from being born and then Baptized. The bride would also sign a promise to abide by her Catholic faith; raise and Baptize her children in the Catholic Church and to bring about the conversion of her "consort."[18]

The New Orleans newspaper, *The Daily Picayune* reported that, "The bride was clad in an exquisite white gown, and approached the altar with her uncle, Mr. J. Walter Hastings.[19] Viola Patterson was accompanied by her uncle as her father was deceased. After the ceremony the bride and groom repaired to the residence of Mr. and Mrs. George W. Barr, No. 1821 Calliope Street, accompanied by her retinue and a large number of guests. Here a magnificent reception was held." The newlyweds "were made the recipients of numerous handsome presents, and also received the congratulations of their legion of friends. Miss Ella Barr was the bridesmaid, and Mr. Marshall Casse the best man. As the happy couple were leaving for their home they were showered with large quantities of rice as well-wishes for a long and contented life. They are temporarily located at No. 1721 St. Charles Avenue, where they will be at home to their many friends."[20]

St. John the Baptist Church

St. John the Baptist Church was built in 1869 on Dryades Street in New Orleans, Louisiana. "The church seats about 1,200 people comfortably, but if its capacious, aisles be used, the seating capacity would be 1,600."[21] "Rev. James P. Malone was the sixth

---

[18] Form: *In Casu Disparitatis Cultus Vel Mixtae Religionis* (In a case of disparity of cult or of a compound of religion), A *Stake in the Land*, by Peter A. Speek, Harper & Brothers Publishers, New York and London, 1921, pp. 189-190
[19] WITCHERT [sic] – PATTERSON, *The Daily Picayune*, New Orleans, LA, April 26, 1903, p. 11
[20] WITCHERT [sic] – PATTERSON, *The Daily Picayune*, New Orleans, LA, April 26, 1903, p. 11
[21] *A Religious Guide and Church Calendar*, St. John the Baptist Church, New Orleans, LA, p. 3, 1908

pastor of St. John the Baptist Church in 1902 and served until his resignation in 1912. Under this enthusiastic direction, the parish glory was revived and activities multiplied."[22] "The church was embellished by frescoing, superb stained-glassed windows and electricity" during Father Malone's rectorship. "The brick work of the building and the tower, are conceded by competent architects, to be the finest in the city."[23] Reverend Father James Malone was born in Canada on September 4, 1868. He was ordained on July 2, 1896 in Hamilton, Ontario. His arrival, incardination into the New Orleans Diocese was in 1896.[24]

Children

Walter and Viola Weichert had three children; two daughters and one son. Helena Mary Weichert was born at home on Havre Street in East Boston, Massachusetts on June 1, 1904.[25] [26] Robert Lawrence Weichert was born on August 3, 1906 at the family's next home on Webster Street in East Boston.[27] Given the same name as her mother, Viola Ruth Weichert was born on

---

[22] *St. John the Baptist Church, A Century of Catholic Parochial Service*, Roger Baudier, SR., K.S.G., Official Chronicler, Archdiocese of New Orleans, LA, 1952

[23] *A Religious Guide and Church Calendar*, St. John the Baptist Church, New Orleans, LA, 1908

[24] Email correspondence, Dorenda Dupont, Archives Staff, Office of Archives and Records Archdiocese, New Orleans, LA

[25] Records inquiry, City of Boston, Registry Department dated May 7, 1908. Pension file no. 925721, Record Group 15; National Archives Bldg., Washington, DC

[26] The Social Security Death Index listed Helena Mary Weichert as "Helena Cecilia Weichert".

[27] Registry Department, City of Boston, MA. May 7, 1908, Walter R. Weichert., Pension file no. 925721, Record Group 15, National Archives Building, Washington, DC

September 18, 1907 in Jersey City, New Jersey[28] and Baptized in the Roman Catholic Parish of St. Anne, Jersey City, on October 13, 1907.[29]

---

[28] Board of Health and Vital Statistics, Hudson County, NJ, May 5, 1908, Walter R. Weichert., Pension file no. 925721. Record Group 15, National Archives Building, Washington, DC

[29] Certificate of Baptism, John J. Maher, Rector, Parish of St. Anne, Walter R. Weichert., Pension file no. 925721, Record Group 15, National Archives Building, Washington, DC

Walter Robert Weichert's Sea Service

Walter Weichert "studied at the New York Nautical College…" After his graduation, the 28 year old was appointed to serve on the collier *Alexander*[30] in 1900[31] as Third Officer.[32] His shipping articles for Third Mate were signed "W.R. Weichert" on August 17, 1900 at New York. He was 5' 9" in height with light complexion and brown eyes.[33]

The United States Naval Collier (U.S.N.C.) *Alexander* was one of several ships that were manned by civilian crews in the Collier Service, a special branch of the U.S. Navy under the Bureau of Navigation. The purpose of these colliers was to supply coal and stores to ships of various fleets and to transport coal to distant fueling stations. The organization of personnel aboard the colliers was similar to that of vessels in the Merchant Service. The Master was the commanding officer on board such ships.[34]

The Certificate of Service, signed by E.D.P. Nickels, Master of the Collier *Alexander*, stated that Walter R. Weichert

---

[30] Weichart [sic] Wedded Here, *The Daily Picayune*, New Orleans, LA, March 8, 1908, p. 4
[31] Form 3-604, Navy Widow's Pension, Regular Establishment, Case 26,707, filed October12, 1908, Pension file no. 925721, Record Group 15; National Archives Bldg., Washington, DC
[32] Transcription of Certificate of Service, dated March 13, 1901, attachment to Form 3-604, Navy Widow's Pension, Regular Establishment, Case 26,707, filed October12, 1908, Pension file no. 925721, Record Group 15; National Archives Bldg., Washington, DC
[33] Correspondence, 4th Endorsement, from W.R. Shoemaker, Commander, U.S. Navy to the Commissioner of Pensions, October 10, 1908, Pension file no. 925721, Record Group 15; National Archives Bldg., Washington, DC
[34] *Regulations for Navy Colliers, Regulations for the Navy Collier Service*, Navy Department, Bureau of Navigation, Government Printing Office, Washington, D.C., 1902, pp. 3, 5

served on the ship during the collier's 6 ½ month voyage from Norfolk to Cavite, Philippines and on the return cruise. Master Nickels wrote, "I found him sober and competent, and as such I can recommend him."[35] Walter Weichert served next as Second Officer on the collier *Hannibal* from 1901 to 1902.[36]

The Naval Auxiliary Service (NAS) was established in 1905 and replaced the Collier Service which was organized in 1898.[37] "The Naval Auxiliary Service as hereby organized will include such transports, supply vessels, colliers, and other vessels as may be assigned to it by the department."[38] The NAS manning was similar to that of vessels in the Merchant Service.

Walter R. Weichert was Second Officer of the United States Auxiliary Service (U.S.A.S.) collier *Brutus* from May 20 to November 30, 1907 during which time he was promoted to First Officer. George M. McDonald, Master of the Brutus wrote, "…he proved himself to be sober, honest and a very efficient and energetic officer." On December 1, 1907 Weichert transferred to the collier *Abarenda*. Master George Worley, U.S.A.S. collier *Abarenda* wrote, "During my acquaintance with Chief Officer Weichert, I found him to be an honest willing and able Officer, and well spoken of by all the Masters under whom he has served." Captain Edward B. Barry, USN, Supervisor of Naval Auxiliaries,

---

[35] Transcription of Certificate of Service, dated March 13, 1901, attachment to Form 3-604, Navy Widow's Pension, Regular Establishment, Case 26,707, filed October12, 1908, Pension file no. 925721, Record Group 15; National Archives Bldg., Washington, DC

[36] Form 3-604, Navy Widow's Pension, Regular Establishment, Case 26,707, filed October12, 1908, Pension file no. 925721, Record Group 15; National Archives Bldg., Washington, DC

[37] Naval Overseas Transportation and Shipping Control, Bureau of Naval Personnel, page 15, March 1949, NAVPERS 10829

[38] Organization, Chapter 1, Part 1, Regulations for the Naval Auxiliary Service, Corrected to January 5, 1910, page 5, Navy Department, Bureau of Navigation, Government Printing Office, Washington, D.C., 1910

wrote of Weichert, "His record has always been very good and excellent."[39]

---

[39] Document, Department of the Navy, Bureau of Navigation, Subject: Bureau of Pensions: Requests descriptive list and history of service and circumstances surrounding the murder of Walter R. Weichert, Chief Officer, killed February 20, 1908, at San Juan, P.R., with endorsements dated March 24, 25, 26, 27, 28, 30, 1908, April 14, 1908, Department of the Navy information to be provided to Bureau of Pensions concerning Walter R. Weichert., Pension file no. 925721, Record Group 15, National Archives Building, Washington, DC

Abarenda's **First Officer**

Sunday, December 1, 1907, 4:00 p.m., Walter R. Weichert reported on board the Naval Auxiliary *Abarenda* which was anchored off the Norfolk and Western Railway coaling piers at Lamberts Point, Norfolk, Virginia. The collier had arrived at 9:00 a.m. that morning from Baltimore, Maryland where she received bunker and cargo coal. Coal stored in a ship's bunker was its own fuel. Cargo coal was provided to other vessels or deposited at coaling stations for later distribution.

"Mr. Witchard", as the ship's logbook erroneously first identified him, replaced T. Foley, two days after his predecessor's discharge, as the *Abarenda's* First Officer.[40] It wasn't long before some of the enlisted men turned against Weichert.

Thursday, December 5, 1907, the *Abarenda* was moored at the Navy Yard, Norfolk, Virginia. "J. Gaudro, [sic] Boatswain came on board drunk and disorderly and was insolent toward 1st Offi [cer]. He was placed in irons and confined to brig."[41]

Saturday, December 7, 1907, the *Abarenda* remained moored at the Navy Yard, Norfolk, Virginia. "Fobinatis, seaman, placed in double irons for using insolent language toward 1st Officer."[42]

On Friday, January 3, 1908 the United States Auxiliary Ship (U.S.A.S.) *Abarenda* arrived at Rio de Janeiro from Norfolk,

---

[40] Log of the United States Naval Auxiliary Abarenda, Record Group 24; National Archives Bldg., Washington, DC
[41] Log of the United States Naval Auxiliary Abarenda, Record Group 24; National Archives Bldg., Washington,
[42] Log of the United States Naval Auxiliary Abarenda, Record Group 24; National Archives Bldg., Washington, DC

Virginia.[43] The *Abarenda* and colliers *Brutus*, *Caesar* and *Nero* had brought coal to that port for the battleship fleet.[44]

On the morning of Wednesday, January 15, 1908, the collier *Abarenda* was moored to the U.S. Navy battleship *Minnesota* for coaling in the harbor at Rio de Janeiro, Brazil. The air temperature was in the 80s by mid-day. At 1:20 p.m., "Seaman Gallagher and Marsden refused to obey lawful orders from 1st Off. threatening to kill same. When taken before the master used violent language, stating that no power on earth could make him turn to.[45] He showed all appearance of drunkenness from alcohol. This is seaman Gallagher's second offense." Both seamen were placed in the brig.[46]

Thursday, January 16, 1908, the *Abarenda* remained moored to the U.S.S. *Minnesota* in the harbor. Coaling of the battleship *Minnesota* resumed early in the morning. At 11:30 a.m., the "Master and 1st Offr. [sic] visited prisoners and found them in the same state of high insubordination, stating that they would incite everyone else if ever let free. Consequently, they were left in confinement." A short time later, "Seaman Chinal and Brewster deliberately disobeyed orders by painting over dirt. Accordingly destroying ship[']s paint and using up ship's time." (L. Chinal was disrated twice during the prior month, from boatswain to quartermaster and from quartermaster to seaman.) "Attention was given to prisoners" at 6:00 p.m. "Seaman Gallagher released from confinement and turned to. Seaman

---

[43] Log of the United States Naval Auxiliary *Abarenda*, Record Group 24; National Archives Bldg., Washington, DC
[44] Coal for the Fleet, Hearst News Service, *The Pensacola Journal*, Pensacola, FL, January 7, 1908, p. 1
[45] Turn to: "An order to commence ship's work." *Naval Terms and Definitions*, Commander C.C. Soule, U.S.N., D. Van Nostrand Company, New York, NY, 1922, p. 70
[46] Log of the United States Naval Auxiliary *Abarenda*, Record Group 24; National Archives Bldg., Washington, DC

Marsden still insubordinate." Marsden remained in the brig; however, "being no longer insubordinate" he was released from irons on January 17, 1908 at 6:30 p.m. He was permitted to return to his duties at 6:00 a.m. on January 18, 1908. Seaman Anderson deserted while ashore on January 20, 1908 as his ship, the *Abarenda* was anchored at Rio de Janeiro harbor. On the morning of January 27, 1908, Seaman Gallagher reported sick and was off duty.[47]

Tuesday, January 28, 1908, the collier *Abarenda* departed Rio de Janeiro, headed for San Juan, Porto Rico.[48] (*"The United States used "Puerto Rico" in diplomatic correspondence before the Spanish-American War but used the anglicized spelling "Porto Rico" in the Treaty of Paris, which ended the conflict."*[49] *Decades later, Congressional legislation would officially change the name of the island back to the original Spanish, "Puerto Rico."*[50]) On the afternoon of January 31, 1908, Seaman Hunter Barnes "was caught in the act of destroying food. This is the fourth offense of same. Is fined ten dollars and shore leave stopped for three months." On Saturday, February 1, 1908, "Deserter Seaman Miller placed in irons and confined to the brig for refusing duty and using insolent language toward commanding officer and chief engineer." An unnamed deserter was "placed in irons and confined to brig for refusing duty. During the time prisoners were released to wash themselves, both locks from brig were destroyed

---

[47] Log of the United States Naval Auxiliary *Abarenda*, Record Group 24; National Archives Bldg., Washington, DC
[48] Log of the United States Naval Auxiliary *Abarenda*, Record Group 24; National Archives Bldg., Washington, DC
[49] *Crafting an Identity*, Office of the Historian: Office of Art & Archives, Office of the Clerk, U.S. House of Representatives, website:
http://history.house.gov/Exhibitions-and-Publications/HAIC/Historical-Essays/Foreign-Domestic/Crafting-Identity/
[50] "S. J. Res. 36. To change the name of the island of "Porto Rico" to "Puerto Rico". Approved May 17, 1932. Public Resolution No. 20". Senate Joint Resolutions, *Calendars of the United States House of Representatives and History of Legislation*, 72nd Congress, Final Edition, March 4, 1933, Clerk of the House of Representatives, U.S. Government Printing Office, Washington, DC, p. 150

or hidden. Suspicion turns toward deserters." The prisoners were released on Monday, February 3, 1908. "Seaman Gallagher unfit for duty on account of venereal disease." On Thursday, February 6, 1908, "Deserter Miller again showed signs of insubordination refusing to work and sharing sickness. Finally turned to again." Saturday, February 8, 1908, "Seaman Gallagher doing light lookout duty refuses to be further treated by the master for venereal disease and demands to mingle with the crew. By orders of the master he is isolated until the boarding of a doctor in next ensuing port."[51]

Wednesday, February 12, 1908, "Seaman L. Chinal stated that his locker had been rifled but on close inspection this was found to be untrue." At 11:30 p.m. that night, H. Castorie, seaman fell down forward companionway ladder and was disabled."[52] *Companion-way, "The steps leading below from the upper deck, usually applied to the hatch reserved for the commanding officer or commander-in-chief."*[53]

Sunday, February 16, 1908, during the midnight to 4:00 a.m. watch, the Naval Auxiliary *Abarenda* arrived from Rio de Janeiro, Brazil and anchored off the Morro Castle, San Juan, Porto

---

[51] Log of the United States Naval Auxiliary *Abarenda*, Record Group 24; National Archives Bldg., Washington, DC
[52] Log of the United States Naval Auxiliary *Abarenda*, Record Group 24; National Archives Bldg., Washington, DC
[53] "Companion-way. The steps leading below from the upper deck, usually applied to the hatch reserved for the commanding officer or commander-in-chief." *Naval Terms and Definitions*, by Commander C.C. Soule, U.S.N., D. Van Nostrand Company, New York, NY, 1922, p. 8

Rico, to await daylight. "U.S.M.H.S.[54] Doctor aboard and placed ship under quarantine."[55]

Monday, February 17, 1908, "J. Goudreau [sic][56], bo's'n [sic] was disrated to seaman for insolent and insulting language toward first officer." Oscar Tyzteman, seaman rated Bo's'n [sic]. The ship remained under quarantine. The crew painted the ship's sides.[57]

Tuesday, February 18, 1908, that morning, "A. Dixon, carpenter, was placed in confinement for deliberately destroying ship's property and using threatening language toward first officer." (Alexander Dickson, ship's carpenter, first appeared in the ship's records as *A. Dixon*[58] and in the San Juan Naval Station communiques, to the Navy Department in Washington, D.C., as *George Dixon*.[59] Based on the Navy's incorrect information, newspapers spread the erroneous name in print.) "U.S.M.H.S. Doctor aboard and declared ship out of quarantine." The crew continued to paint the ship's side. That afternoon, the *Abarenda*

---

[54] U.S.M.H.S - United States Marine Hospital Service, authorized July 1798 by "An Act for the relief of sick and disabled Seamen". Later reorganized as the U.S Public Health Service. website: http://history.nih.gov, Office of History and Stetten Museum, National Institutes of Health, Bethesda, MD
[55] Log of the United States Naval Auxiliary *Abarenda*, Record Group 24; National Archives Bldg., Washington, DC
[56] Goodro, John; Correct spelling per court documents, Case File 408; Criminal Case Files; U.S. District Court for the District of Puerto Rico; Records of District Courts of the United States, Record Group 21; National Archives at New York City.
[57] Log of the United States Naval Auxiliary *Abarenda*, Record Group 24; National Archives Bldg., Washington, DC
[58] Log of the United States Naval Auxiliary *Abarenda*, Record Group 24; National Archives Bldg., Washington, DC
[59] Commodore, Karl Rohrer (retired), Commandant, Naval Station, San Juan, PR to Bureau of Navigation, Washington, D.C., February 20, 1908; p. 344, San Juan Naval Station Cablegrams, Entry 739, Records of Naval Station San Juan, P.R., Naval Districts and Shore Establishments, Record Group 181; National Archives and Records Administration - Northeast Region, New York City

moored alongside the San Juan Naval Station's dock where Marines took charge of deserters; one was placed in the hospital.[60]

Wednesday, February 19, 1908, "Carpenter released from confinement being carefully watched as he is suspected of deliberately destroying." The crew continued to paint the ship's side. The *Abarenda* took on 31 packages of freight. "One case fell out of slings and [was] completely broken, none of her contents lost. The accident was due to bad slinging by Bo's'n Tyzteman. Two of *Abarenda's* seamen manned her coaling winches as the "shore gang" coaled the ship.[61]

On Thursday, February 20, 1908, 12:50 p.m., "Carpenter Dixon deliberately refusing 1st Officer's orders such to be referred to Norfolk Navy Yard."[62] "Between 1:00 and 1:05 p.m. First Off [sic] W. R. Weichert was killed with an axe in the hands of Alex Dixon, ship's carpenter. Dixon immediately gave himself up to the Third Officer saying he had killed the First Officer and handing over the axe with which it was done. Dixon was taken in charge by marine from the Naval Station. About 2:30 p.m. Board of Inquest met aboard the ship…"[63] Members of the Board of Inquest: J. A. Bell, Commander, U.S. Navy, Retired, President; U.R, Webb, P. A. Surgeon, U.S. Navy, Member; F. Halford, 1st Lieutenant, U.S.M.C., Member; G. Freudendorf, Chief Boatswain, U.S. Navy, Recorder.[64]

---

[60] Log of the United States Naval Auxiliary *Abarenda*, Record Group 24; National Archives Bldg., Washington, DC
[61] Log of the United States Naval Auxiliary *Abarenda*, Record Group 24; National Archives Bldg., Washington, DC
[62] Log of the United States Naval Auxiliary *Abarenda*, Record Group 24; National Archives Bldg., Washington, DC
[63] Log of the United States Naval Auxiliary *Abarenda*, Record Group 24; National Archives Bldg., Washington, DC
[64] Extracts from Record of proceedings of a Board of Inquest convened on board the U.S.A.S. Abarenda in the case of Walter R. Weichert, Chief Officer, February 20, 1908. Record Group 233; National Archives Building, Washington, DC

Karl Rohrer, Commandant, Naval Station, San Juan, P.R., telegrammed the Navy Department, Bureau of Navigation, Washington, D.C., "George Dixon, Carpenter killed Walter Weichert, Chief Officer Abarenda today." The Commandant followed that message with another to the Bureau of Navigation, "District Attorney advises Dixon, four witnesses, submitted Grand Jury meeting April. Request instructions."[65]

The U.S.A.S. *Abarenda* was in service at that time; not in commission. The collier was manned by civilian officers and crew who were employed by the Naval Auxiliary Service. The court martial process was not applicable.

"Extracts from Record of Proceedings of a Board of Inquest convened on board the U.S.A.S. Abarenda in the case of Walter R. Weichert, Chief Officer, February 20, 1908

Testimony of Harry M. Bostwick, third officer, U.S.A.S. Abarenda

A.5. Just before one o'clock on February 20th, 1908, I was sent for by the deceased to come into the wheel-house. When I reached there Mr. Weichert was there with carpenter Dickson. I was asked to read an entry which was made in the rough log by the Chief Officer and told to sign my name to it. The entry in question consisted as follows, "Carpenter Dickson deliberately refusing first officer's orders, such to be referred to Norfolk Navy Yard". Signed by W. R. Weichert and myself. After I signed the log the

---

[65] Commodore, Karl Rohrer (retired), Commandant, Naval Station, San Juan, PR to Bureau of Navigation, Washington, D.C., February 20, 1908; p. 344, San Juan Naval Station Cablegrams, Entry 739, Records of Naval Station San Juan, P.R., Naval Districts and Shore Establishments, Record Group 181; National Archives and Records Administration - Northeast Region, New York City

carpenter was sent below and I went to the chart room and laid down on the couch. A little while later when two bells was struck I heard a noise forward which appeared to be rather unusual. I got up and went forward to the berth deck companionway. Before I reached there the noise had stopped and I met the carpenter coming out of the companionway with an axe in his hand and he laid the axe on number two hatch, held out his hands and said to me "put me in irons, I have killed the mate" or words to that effect. He had blood on his hands and there was blood on the axe and he looked excited. I then called the boatswain who was nearby to take charge of carpenter Dickson and I told the quartermaster to run for the doctor and came aft to get irons but could find no keys, so ran on to the dock and got the marines and hospital steward.

Testimony of William Easton, seaman, U.S.A.S. Abarenda.

A.5.- About one p.m. on February 20th, 1908, I saw the chief Officer W. R. Weichert and carpenter Dickson on the bridge of this ship. I heard the Chief Officer say something to the carpenter, but did not understand the words. Then the carpenter went down the companionway leading to the forward berth deck. Then the Chief Officer followed the carpenter down. A few minutes afterwards, just as soon as the Chief Officer went down, I heard a shouting. I went to the companionway and saw the Chief Officer on the deck and the carpenter on top of him. I then left the companionway to notify the third officer of what was going on forward. After I had gone about twenty feet I heard the Chief Officer shouting for help and I turned back and went again to the companionway and looked down and I saw the axe underneath the Chief Officer's chest. Then I went down the companionway and saw the Chief Officers clothing full of blood and the Chief Officer laying on deck. The Chief Officer then told me to get the third officer. I ran up on deck using the port companionway ladder. The third officer was then by the hatch on the starboard side. Then I went down the companionway again and I saw a cut on the Chief Officer's neck. Carpenter Dickson was standing beside the body of the Chief Officer and he had an axe in his hand. The carpenter then went up on deck carrying the axe with him. I followed him on deck. Meeting the third officer on deck, the carpenter said to the third officer "I have killed the mate sir", throwing the axe down. I then stayed with carpenter Dickson who was walking aft meanwhile. A little while later a marine guard from the Station took charge of carpenter Dickson.

Q.6.- Where any remarks made by carpenter Dickson when you followed him aft, and just previous to his arrest by the Marine Guard of this Station?

A.6.- Yes sir.

Q.7.- State the nature of these remarks.

A.7.- The carpenter said that he would allow no man to call him a bastard or disgrace his father or mother. He also said that he would not go over the side on the stage.[66]

Q.8.- Where were you when you heard the shouting.

A.8.- 1 was forward sir, about 18 or 19 yards from the hatch.

Q.9.- Tell in detail what you first saw when you looked down the companionway?

A.9.- The mate was lying on the deck and the carpenter was on top of him.

Q.10.- Did the carpenter have anything in his hands at that time?

A.10.- No sir he did not, he had his hands around the Chief Officer's neck.

Q.11.- When you went down the hatch the first time the chief Officer asked you to call the third officer, did you leave immediately afterwards?

A.11.- I did.

---

[66] "Stage. A plank platform, or single plank used to support men while working." "Hanging stage, a stage suspended over the ship's side." *A Naval Encyclopædia*, L.R. Hamersly & Co., Philadelphia, PA, 1884 (Republished by Gale Research Co., Detroit, 1971), p. 771

Q.12.- Where was the carpenter and what was he doing when you went down, the first time?
A.12.- He was still on top of him and I then saw a lot of blood on the chief officer's clothing.
Q.13.- Did you hear the chief officer say anything on your second visit?
A.13.- No sir, I did not.
Q.14.- Did you see the carpenter do anything with the axe?
A.14.- No sir, I did not.
Q.15.- Whose chest was the axe under?
A.15.- The chief officer's chest.
Q.16.- Are you sure that the chief officer spoke to you when you went down the first time?
A.16.- Yes sir.
Q.17.- Was there anyone else on the berth deck when you went down, except the carpenter and the first officer?
A.17.- No sir, only myself.

There being no further questions to ask this witness his testimony was read over to him, and by him pronounced to be correct, whereupon he withdrew.

P. A. Surgeon Webb, U.R, U. S. Navy, states that in his opinion the deceased came to his death as a result of three wounds inflicted with some sharp heavy instrument, one wound situated just below poupart[']s ligament across the right thigh was about five inches long, very deep, and had severed the femoral artery. The other two wounds joined at the extremities and extended from midway between the angle of the mouth and the ear on the left side to beyond the middle of the back of the neck. These wounds had severed the left lower jaw carotid artery and the spinal cord at the base of the brain.
Q.1.- Could such wounds have been inflicted by an axe?
A.1.- Yes.

Q.2.- Can you state the probable sequence in which these wounds were inflicted, and if so, give your reasons?
A.2.- It is probable that the wound in the thigh was the first one inflicted, The other two must have been inflicted some minutes later, as there was very little hemorrhage from the two wounds in the neck. While there had been profuse hemorrhage from the wound in the thigh. It is probable that the wounds in the neck were inflicted after the body had fallen.

The proceedings closed here.

The Board, from a view of the body, and from the evidence before it is of the opinion that W. R. Weichert, Chief Officer, U. S. A. S. Abarenda, came to his death through wounds inflicted by an axe in the hands of Alexander Dickson, carpenter of the U. S. A. S. Abarenda, and that his death occurred in the line of duty."[67]

"Board of Inquest adjourned at 4-45 having completed their labors. The body of First Offi [sic] W.R. Weichert was taken charge of by U.R. Webb, Surgeon, U.S.N. and removed to the dispensary of the Naval Station to be prepared for interment. Colors set at half mast during the afternoon. No work done by the coal gang during the afternoon. Crew was engaged in painting the ships sides."[68]

A few weeks later, the Brooklyn, New York newspaper, *Brooklyn Daily Eagle*, included information from an unidentified source to report that at 9:00 a.m. on the morning of February 20th, Alexander Dickson, who was alleged to have been a deserter from the British Navy, "was paid off by the captain and told that he could have shore leave. Instead of going on shore however, it seems that he extracted an ax from its rack between the decks and

---

[67] Extracts from Record of proceedings of a Board of Inquest convened on board the U.S.A.S. *Abarenda* in the case of Walter R. Weichert, Chief Officer, February 20, 1908. Records of the United States House of Representatives, Record Group 233; National Archives Building, Washington, DC
[68] Log of the United States Naval Auxiliary *Abarenda*, Record Group 24; National Archives Bldg., Washington, DC

spent about three hours sharpening it to a razor-like keenness. It took him all of that time, for ship's axes are never ground to an edge. They are thoroughly shellaced [sic] and are never taken from their racks unless the captain calls for a fire drill. When the ax had been sharpened, Dickson took up a position alongside of the gangway leading from the forward deck to the berth deck below. As his body came on a line with the level of Dickson's shoulders, the murderer swung the ax and brought it down on Weichert's groin, almost completely severing the left leg from the body. The victim toppled down the ladder without a groan. One of the sailors witnessed the attack and went to summon help. In the meantime, Dickson maddened by the sight of blood, wielded his ax a second and third time, cleaving his victim's head and almost separating it from the body. By the time help arrived, Dickson was completely exhausted by his fiendish work. He was captured and disarmed without difficulty and placed in irons."[69] A United Press dispatch stated, "The blow was so violent that Weichert's head only clung to his trunk by a thread of skin."[70]

More than a month after the murder, Master George Worley recalled, "W.R. Weichert served on the U.S.S. ABARENDA, as Chief Officer under my command from the 1st December, to the 20th February 1908, when he was cruelly murdered by Aleck Dickson, a carpenter with an axe, while said officer was intending to perform ship's duties. The murder took place at about noon, while the ship was alongside the Navy Yard, receiving bunker coal. I was on shore when the murder occurred, therefore cannot give but a meagre description of what took place, only that I was informed that the carpenter had cut the Chief

---

[69] First Officer Slain in Naval Auxiliary, *The Brooklyn Daily Eagle*, Brooklyn, NY, March 11, 1908, p. 20
[70] Murder Committed, *Laredo Times*, Laredo, TX, February 23, 1908, p. 11

officer's head off with an axe." /signed/ Geo. Worley, Master, N.A.S. [71]

The ladder on the *Abarenda* would have been inclined not vertical. The axe used in the murder would likely have been a fire axe; an item located at specific stations, secured by latches, on the ship. One location may have been near the access to the engineering section. The axes were there for safety purposes and to cut lines.[72]

Official Report of Death

The undated Report of Death form was filed by P. A. Surgeon U.R. Webb, U. S. Navy, signed by Master Worley (commanding U.S.A.S. *Abarenda*) and approved by Commodore, Karl Rohrer, Commandant, San Juan Naval Station. Date, time and place of death: February 20, 1908, 1:10 p.m., U.S.A.S *Abarenda*. Deceased: Walter R. Weichert, Chief Officer (Collier), 36 years of age, 5' 9" tall, dark complexion, black hair, brown eyes. The cause of death: "Hemorrhage, and severance of spinal cord." "The deceased received three wounds inflicted with an ax. One of these laid open his right thigh, just above Poupart's ligament and severed the femoral artery, another laid open his left cheek and side of neck, severing the carotid artery, the other severed the spinal cord at the base of the brain. Death must have been instantaneous."[73]

---

[71] 3rd Endorsement, George Worley, Master, *Abarenda*, Navy Yard, Brooklyn, N.Y., March 26, 1908, Subject. Bureau of pensions: Requests descriptive list and history of service, and circumstances surrounding the murder of Walter R. Weichert, chief officer, killed February 20, 1908, at San Juan, P.R.
[72] Author's conversation with Mark L. Evans, Historian, Ships History Branch, Naval History & Heritage Command, Washington Navy Yard, August 28, 2012
[73] Report of Death, Walter R. Weichert, Chief Officer, Form N, Bureau of Medicine and Surgery, Navy Department, February 20, 1908, Pension file no.

Friday, February 21, 1908, the collier *Abarenda* remained moored alongside the United States Naval Station dock, San Juan, P.R. At 8:30 a.m., a "Party of three seamen and three firemen left ship in charge of Bo's'n H.A. Stanley U.S.N.[74] for the purpose of digging grave for the body of First Off'r [sic]W.R. Weichert, deceased." The weather conditions, 82 degrees, gentle breeze, clear blue sky with a few cumulus clouds aloft. The ship's log stated that the "Deceased First Off'r [sic] W.R. Weichert was buried by order of the Commandant at 2:00 P.M. with all the honors due to a Naval Officer. He was buried in Naval Graveyard outside of San Juan, P.R."[75] The official U.S. Navy *burial* register stated that his place of burial was in grave 204 of the San Juan Military Cemetery. It listed Walter R, Weichert's cause of death as "hemorrhage & severance of spinal cord."[76]

Back in the states, news of the killing spread like wildfire via the wire services, such as United Press[77] and Associated Press,[78] to newspapers from coast to coast. Articles, not for the timid, quickly appeared bearing titles such as: "Bloody Crime on Vessel"[79] "Mate of Collier Murdered"[80] "Severed Officer's

---

925721, Records of the Veterans Administration, Record Group 15, National Archives Bldg., Washington, DC

[74] Henry Aloysius Stanley, Boatswain, U.S.N., Naval Station, San Juan, assigned April 2, 1907, *Register of the Commissioned and Warrant Officers of the United States Navy and Marine Corps*, Government Printing Office, Washington, DC, January 1, 1908, p. 90

[75] Log of the United States Naval Auxiliary *Abarenda*, Record Group 24; National Archives Bldg., Washington, DC

[76] Register of Dead, Naval Hospital, San Juan, PR, p. 3, Record Group 52; National Archives Bldg., Washington, DC

[77] Murder Committed, *Laredo Times*, Laredo, TX, February 23, 1908, p. 11

[78] Severed Officer's Head, *Daily Free Press*, Carbondale, IL, February 21, 1908, p. 1

[79] Bloody Crime on Vessel, *La Crosse Tribune*, La Crosse, WI, February 21, 1908, p. 5

[80] Mate of Collier Murdered, *The Sun*, Baltimore, MD, February 21, 1908, p. 5

Head"[81] and more. No ink was spared in the daily coverage of the story with all its grisly details. Accuracy in print varied between publications. While most of the titles appeared with bold capital letters, the *Denver Post* carried a story in which the sensational title, "Naval Officer Slain With Ax"[82] was almost as large as the article itself. This was undoubtedly an event made for the tabloids; however, no crime-scene images were carried by the newspapers. In its Sunday edition, 16 days after the murder, the *Times-Picayune* of New Orleans published a formal photo of Walter R. Weichert in his Naval Auxiliary Service uniform.[83]

Mrs. Viola Weichert received a letter of sympathy at her home in Jersey City Heights, N.J, "on account of the death of her husband,"[84] from the Assistant Supervisor of Naval Auxiliaries, De Witt Clinton Redgrave, Commander, U.S.N., Retired.[85] The letter stated "that her husband was buried with military honors in the cemetery at San Juan."[86]

Master Worley raised approximately $500 for the benefit of Mrs. Weichert. Contributions came from the crews of the colliers *Abarenda*, *Brutus* and *Nero*.[87]

Monday, February 24, 1908, The *Abarenda* was moored alongside the Naval Station dock at San Juan, Porto Rico. The U.S. Marshal arrived on board and subpoenaed 17 members of the

---

[81] Severed Officer's Head, *Daily Free Press*, Carbondale, IL, February 21, 1908, p 1
[82] Naval Officer Slain With Ax, *The Denver Post*, Denver, CO, February 21, 1908, p. 8
[83] Weichart [sic] Wedded Here, *The Daily Picayune*, New Orleans, LA, March 8, 1908, p. 4
[84] Weichart [sic] Wedded Here, *The Daily Picayune*, New Orleans, LA, March 8, 1908, p. 4
[85] Retired List, *Register of the Commissioned and Warrant Officers of the United States Navy and Marine Corps*, Navy Department, U.S. Government Printing Office, Washington, DC, January 1, 1908, p. 152
[86] Weichart [sic] Wedded Here, *The Daily Picayune*, New Orleans, LA, March 8, 1908, p. 4
[87] First Officer Slain in Naval Auxiliary, *The Brooklyn Daily Eagle*, Brooklyn, NY, March 11, 1908, p. 20

crew who had appeared before the U.S. District Court: P.M. Gadeberg, 2nd Officer; H.M. Bostwick, 3rd Officer; Anthony Kelley 1st Assistant Engineer; Mark H. Winner 2nd Assistant Engineer; H B. Beebe 3rd Assistant Engineer; J. Gaudro Seaman; J.W. Sutton, Electrician; O. Fyskman, Boatswain; J. Gustafsin, Quartermaster; S. Bonnano, Quartermaster; P. Gallagher, Seaman; A. De La Fonte, Fireman; L. Brewer, Seaman; T.H. Barnes, Seaman; J. Marsden, Seaman;[88][sic] L. Chinal, Seaman; W. Easton, Seaman. Those men were held under $500.00 bail to appear before the court on April 13, 1908 as witnesses in the case of United States v. Alexander Dickson. Being unable to post bail, most persons named were detained ashore for "safe keeping" by the U.S. Marshal. Second Officer P.M. Gadeberg and Third Officer H.M. Bostwick were permitted to stay by the ship on their own personal recognizances to appear on said date.[89]

A message, dated February 24, 1908, was prepared for transmission under Commander Rohrer's signature, but was stricken. The word "Void" was handwritten in red sideways across the page from bottom to top. In it, Rohrer stated that the *Abarenda* was ready to depart and that the U.S. Commissioner held the "murderer, first officer and 17 of the crew". He inquired of the Bureau of Navigation, "Shall vessel remain here until trial [in] April or shall I fill her crew sufficiently [to] continue [her] voyage [with men] from Brutus and Nero."[90]

---

[88] Marsden, George; Correct spelling per court documents, Case File 408; Criminal Case Files; U.S. District Court for the District of Puerto Rico; Records of District Courts of the United States, Record Group 21; National Archives at New York City.
[89] Log of the United States Naval Auxiliary *Abarenda*, Record Group 24; National Archives Bldg., Washington, DC
[90] Commodore, Karl Rohrer (retired), Commandant, Naval Station, San Juan, PR to Bureau of Navigation, Washington, D.C., February 24, 1908; p. 346, San Juan Naval Station Cablegrams, Entry 739, Records of Naval Station San Juan, P.R.,

February 25, 1908, The *Abarenda* was anchored in San Juan Harbor. The effects and clothing of the detained members of the crew were taken ashore under the supervision of two U.S. Marshals.[91] The Navy Department, Washington, D.C. advised the San Juan Naval Station, "Telegram stating seventeen witnesses detained from Abarenda Dixon case received. Confer with district attorney relative reducing such witnesses so as not to cripple movements of ship. Wire action." - V. H. Metcalf, Secretary.[92] Dickson went before the United States Commissioner. Many witnesses testified that Weichert had treated Dickson brutally when he was a prisoner and placed him in irons. They had many quarrels. Dickson was remanded to the Grand Jury that day.[93]

February 26, 1908, Commander Rohrer's questions, from two days prior, were answered. A Quartermaster, two Seamen, and a Second Assistant Engineer from the U.S.S. *Nero*; and a Quartermaster, two Seamen, and a First Assistant Engineer from the U.S.S. *Brutus*, reported on board the *Abarenda* for duty. Under the command of Master Worley, the collier *Abarenda* departed San Juan at 1:40 p.m , en route to Norfolk, Virginia.[94] Commander Rohrer advised the Bureau of Navigation, Washington, "Abarenda, Brutus Hampton-Roads 26th."[95]

February 27, 1908, Commodore Rohrer, Commandant, Naval Station, San Juan, Porto Rico, advised the Secretary of the

---

Naval Districts and Shore Establishments, Record Group 181; National Archives and Records Administration - Northeast Region, New York City
[91] Log of the United States Naval Auxiliary *Abarenda*, Record Group 24; National Archives Bldg., Washington, DC
[92] Telegram No. 7204-2, Victor H. Metcalf, Secretary of the Navy to Naval Station, San Juan, P.R., February 25, 1908, Record Group 181; National Archives and Records Administration - Northeast Region, New York City
[93] ABARENDA Murder Hearing, *The Sun*, New York, NY, February 26, 1908, p. 1
[94] Log of the United States Naval Auxiliary *Abarenda*, Record Group 24; National Archives Bldg., Washington, DC
[95] Cablegrams from Commodore, Karl Rohrer (retired), Commandant, Naval Station, San Juan, PR, to Navy Department, Washington, DC, February 26, 1908, p. 347, Record Group 181; National Archives and Records Administration - Northeast Region, New York City

Navy, via telegram, that he "Conferred District Attorney and Counsel Defense Dickson case. Former six witnesses, two paroled own recognizance, Defense thirteen. Insist holding. Two are naval stragglers."[96]

That same day, Rear Admiral William C. Cowles, Chief, Bureau of Equipment, telegraphed the San Juan Naval Station, "Handschlag load abarenda newriver coal."[97] Although that message appeared to be a combination of German and misspellings of other words, it's actually a partially coded message. The term "handschlag" comes from the Western Union Telegraphic Code.[98] That code provided ways to save the cost of sending messages via commercial telegraph companies and if needed, could offer basic communications security. In this case, "handschlag" was code for "As soon as ready." One term served to convey 4 words of a phrase. The term "newriver", while not a code term is simply two words that were merged. Translated, the message stated: As soon as ready, load Abarenda [with] New River coal, from the New River District, [Beckley Bed at West Raleigh,] West Virginia. New River coal was coal was a low

---

[96] Cablegrams from Commodore, Karl Rohrer (retired), Commandant, Naval Station, San Juan, PR, to Navy Department, Washington, DC, February 27, 1908, Record Group 181; National Archives and Records Administration - Northeast Region, New York City

[97] Telegram (handwritten on West India and Panama Telegraph Company, Limited form) prior to typing at receiving end) from Rear Admiral William C. Cowles, Chief, Bureau of Equipment, Washington, DC to the San Juan Naval Station, February 27, 1908, San Juan Naval Station Letters Received by Commandant, Entry 732, Records of Naval Station San Juan, P.R., Naval Districts and Shore Establishments, Record Group 181; National Archives and Records Administration - Northeast Region, New York City

[98] Term: "Handschlag", *Western Union Telegraphic Code*, Universal Edition, Compiled and Published by International Cable Directory Company, New York, NY, 1903, p. 362

volatile bituminous or semi-bituminous coal in character; very friable (easily crumbled or pulverized[99]).[100]

March 10, 1908, The *Abarenda* arrived at the Brooklyn, New York Navy Yard[101] "…with her crew partly augmented from detachments from both the Nero and Brutus. She will remain here for a fortnight during which time she will undergo minor repairs in dry dock and then leave for San Juan to pick up that portion of her crew which was detained for the trial." "His home [Master George W. Worley] is in Seattle, Wash. To-morrow he expects his wife here with a seven month old daughter. The captain's wife and child have been nearly a week on their journey across the country." "I wouldn't have her come such a long way," said the captain in the morning, "but I'm anxious to see my daughter. I have not seen as yet at all. She was born while I was out at sea.""[102]

March 23, 1908 at noon, the Naval Auxiliary *Abarenda* was alongside a dock at the Navy Yard, Brooklyn, New York. "Capt. Geo. Worley was put in furlough and relieved of command of the ship by Capt. W. Fincke."[103] Master Worley's command of the *Abarenda* commenced on June 1, 1907.[104]

---

[99] Friable, *Webster's Secondary-School Dictionary*, G & C Merriam Co., Springfield, MA, 1913, p. 289
[100] Comparative Tests of Coal and Briquettes On U. S. Torpedo Boat *Biddle*, Department of the Interior, United States Geological Survey, Bulletin 363, Comparative Tests of Run-Of-Mine and Briquetted Coal on Locomotives By W. F. M. Goss, Washington Government Printing Office, 1908, p. 46
[101] Log of the United States Naval Auxiliary *Abarenda*, Record Group 24; National Archives Bldg., Washington, DC
[102] First Officer Slain in Naval Auxiliary, *The Brooklyn Daily Eagle*, Brooklyn, NY, March 11, 1908, p. 20
[103] Log of the United States Naval Auxiliary *Abarenda*, Record Group 24; National Archives Bldg., Washington, DC
[104] U.S.S. ABARENDA, ZC File, May 9, 1951, Naval History & Heritage Command, Washington Navy Yard, Washington, DC

The District Court of the United States for Porto Rico

Bernard S. Rodey, Judge

Bernard Shandon Rodey was born on March 1, 1856, in County Mayo, Ireland. Rodey worked as a stenographer and as a as a court reporter for the second district of New Mexico in 1882. The following year he was admitted to the practice of law. In 1883 he founded the Rodey Law Firm (Rodey, Dickason, Sloan, Akin and Robb, P.A.). which operates today in Santa Fe and Albuquerque, New Mexico. Early on, he was a criminal defense attorney, focused on the underdogs and the poor. Elected to the territorial legislature from Bernalillo County in 1888, he served for a single term. In 1900 and again in 1902 he was elected to serve in the U.S. House of Representatives where he advocated for statehood for New Mexico, Arizona and Oklahoma. He failed to keep his Congressional seat following the election of 1904.[105] He was appointed by President Theodore Roosevelt as United States District Judge[106] for Porto Rico at San Juan on June 15, 1906[107] at an annual salary of $5,000.[108] In 1910, Judge Rodey was replaced; however President Taft appointed Judge Rodey to serve as the U.S. Attorney for the Second Division, Territory of Alaska. On March 6, 1912, Judge Rodey was appointed special assistant U.S.

---

[105] United States District Court for the District of Puerto Rico, website http://www.prd.uscourts.gov/?q=node/190
[106] United States District Court for the District of Puerto Rico, website http://www.prd.uscourts.gov/?q=node/190
[107] *List of United States Judges, Attorneys, and Marshals*, Compiled by the Appointment Clerk, Department of Justice, July 1, 1909, Government Printing Office, Washington, DC, p. 18
[108] Courts of Porto Rico, *Official Register, Persons in the Civil, Military and Naval Service of the United States, and List of Vessels*, Volume 1 Directory, Compiled by the Department of Commerce and Labor Bureau of the Census, Government Printing Office, Washington, DC, 1909, p. 114

Attorney, Western District of Washington where he served until 1913. That year Judge Rodey returned to Albuquerque and resumed the private practice of law. He died in Albuquerque on March 10, 1927, age, 71.[109]

José R.F. Savage, United States Attorney

José Ramon Fernandez Savage was born in New York City, N.Y. on September 29, 1873.[110] On March 18, 1901 he was appointed judge for the District Court of San Juan.[111] He was appointed by the President [Theodore Roosevelt][112] as the United States Attorney for the District of Porto Rico at San Juan on December 19, 1906[113] at an annual salary of $4,000.[114] Starting in July 1908 and into the 1920s, José R.F. Savage was an attorney with the New York City-based law firm of Curtis, Mallet, Prevost and Colt for which he traveled extensively in Europe, South America and the Dominican Republic. In December 1922, Judge Savage took temporary charge of the Rio de Janeiro, Brazil office

---

[109] United States District Court for the District of Puerto Rico, website http://www.prd.uscourts.gov/?q=node/190

[110] National Archives and Records Administration (NARA); Washington D.C.; NARA Series: Passport Applications, January 2, 1906 - March 31, 1925; Roll #: 172; Volume #: Roll 0172 - Certificates: 83529-84480, 22 Oct 1912-15 Nov 1912

[111] *First Annual Report of Charles H. Allen, Governor of Porto Rico*, May 1, 1901, Government Printing Office, Washington, DC, p. 117

[112] News of the Profession, *Law Notes*, Edward Thompson Company, Northport, LI, NY, January 1907, p. 196

[113] *List of United States Judges, Attorneys, and Marshals*, Compiled by the Appointment Clerk, Department of Justice, July 1, 1909, Government Printing Office, Washington, DC, p. 21

[114] Courts of Porto Rico, *Official Register, Persons in the Civil, Military and Naval Service of the United States, and List of Vessels*, Volume 1 - Directory, Compiled by the Department of Commerce and Labor Bureau of the Census, Government Printing Office, Washington, DC, 1909, p. 114

of Curtis, Mallet, Prevost and Colt.[115] José R.F. Savage died in May 1939.[116]

---

[115] National Archives and Records Administration (NARA); Washington D.C.; NARA Series: Passport Applications, January 2, 1906 - March 31, 1925; Roll #: 2151; Volume #: Roll 2151 - Certificates: 237976-238349, 18 Dec 1922-20 Dec 1922

[116] Green-Wood Cemetery, Brooklyn, NY, website http://www.green-wood.com/

Carpenter Dickson's Trial

United States v. Alexander Dickson[117]
San Juan, Criminal, No. 403, Manslaughter,
Violation of Revised Statute 5341

In the District Court of the United States for Porto Rico

Judge of the District Court of the United States for Porto Rico -
Bernard Shandon Rodey

United States Attorney - José R.F. Savage

Attorneys for defendant:
Mr. William H. Hawkins and Mr. Joseph Anderson

Petit Jurors:
J.A. Canals (Jury Foreman), C.P. Avery, T.J. Case, Jr., H.J. Caul, B. Conelly, John Garden, A. Holst, Robert L. Junghanns, G.S. Lathrop, N.P. Nichols, J.M Turner, Lucas P. Valdiviso

Chronology

March 18, 1908 – Entering return of indictment by Grand Jury (Clerk's fee $0.15). Filing of indictment (Clerk's fee $0.10).
March 19, 1908 – Defendant arraigned and given until March 21st at 2 p.m. to plead.
March 21, 1908 – Plea to jurisdiction filed, heard and overruled. Defendant arraigned and pleads not guilty.
March 25, 1908 – Præcipe[118] for witnesses for government filed

---

[117] U.S. vs. Alexander Dickson, pp. 520 - 526; Criminal Record, p. 1; Criminal Docket; U.S. District Court for the District of Puerto Rico; Records of District Courts of the United States, Record Group 21; National Archives at New York City.

[118] Præcipe – Definition: An original writ commanding the defendant to do something or show cause to the contrary. *A Concise Law Dictionary of Words,*

and subpoena issued.
March 28, 1908 – Præcipe for witnesses for defendant filed and subpoena issued.
March 30, 1908 – Præcipe for witnesses for defendant filed and subpoena issued. Subpoena for plaintiff and subpoena for defendant filed. Motion to quash filed, considered and overruled. Præcipe for witness for defendant filed and subpoena issued for defendant. Jury Sworn and part of testimony heard.
March 31, 1908 – Præcipe for witness for U.S. filed, but witnesses appeared without service. Præcipe for witness for U.S. filed and subpoena issued, served and filed. Subpoena for witnesses for defendant filed, served. Testimony concluded. Argument of Counsel and charge of Court heard. Jury renders verdict of not guilty. Defendant discharged.
April 1, 1908 – Præcipe for discharge of witnesses filed.
April 2, 1908 – Præcipe for discharge of witnesses filed.
April 10, 1908 – Præcipe for discharge of witnesses filed.
April 11, 1908 – In leaving receipts therefor, W.H. Hawkins is permitted to withdraw certain photographs introduced in evidence in this case.

Prior to the Dickson petit jury trial, counsel filed a plea regarding the Court's jurisdiction which was overruled.[119] "Federal courts have jurisdiction to try cases of manslaughter charged to have been committed upon waters within the admiralty jurisdiction of the court."[120]

Although a verbatim transcript of the Dickson trial is not among the many surviving documents of that federal court case, a summary of the trial, published in the *Porto Rico Federal*

Phrases and Maxims, By Frederic Jesup Stimson, Revised by Harvey Cortlandt Voorhees, Little, Brown and Company, Boston 1911, p. 282

[119] U.S. vs. Alexander Dickson, pp. 520 - 526; Criminal Record, p. 1; Criminal Docket; U.S. District Court for the District of Puerto Rico; Records of District Courts of the United States, Record Group 21; National Archives at New York City

[120] United States v. Alexander Dickson, *Porto Rico Federal Reports,* Honorable Henry F. Hord, Reporter, The Lawyers Co-Operative Publishing Company, Rochester, NY., 1909, p. 116

Reports,[121] the following year, provided important insight. During the trial, statements of fact were developed from the evidence. The late Walter R. Weichert was characterized as a provocative officer with a violent temper and an ongoing grudge against Dickson. The only witness to the deed was Alexander Dickson, himself, who testified that, in self-defense he grabbed the axe from the officer who cursed him and planned to use it "to fix him…"[122]

Thirteen days earlier, a grand jury indicted Alexander Dickson of manslaughter, not murder. We were not in the court with either the grand or petit juries and therefore have only a limited understanding of what scenario, evidence or statements presented under oath brought either assembly of jurors to render their indictment and verdict.

Statement to the Petit Jury by Bernard S. Rodey, Judge[123]

"The facts developed by the evidence were about as follows: Deceased was a mate of the ship, was very overbearing and irascible, had for several days exhibited violent temper toward defendant, and had "logged" him on the ship's register for very trivial delinquencies, and threatened him with bodily injury. On the day of the homicide, deceased provoked a quarrel or two with defendant, apparently without any sufficient reason therefor, and finally ordered him to do some painting on the outside of the ship, which defendant, who was a carpenter, considered was no part of his duty, and instead of obeying the order, went below to work at his carpenter's bench. A moment or two later deceased followed

---

[121] *Porto Rico Federal Reports*, Vol. IV, Honorable Henry F. Hord, Reporter, the Lawyer's Co-Operative Publishing company, Rochester, NY, 1909, pp 116-124
[122] United States v. Alexander Dickson, *Porto Rico Federal Reports*, Honorable Henry F. Hord, Reporter, The Lawyers Co-Operative Publishing Company, Rochester, NY., 1909, p. 117
[123] *Porto Rico Federal Reports*, Vol. IV, Honorable Henry F. Hord, Reporter, the Lawyer's Co-Operative Publishing company, Rochester, NY, 1909, pp 116-124

him below. The evidence of defendant, who was the only eyewitness, was that deceased came down the companionway, rushed to the carpenter's bench, secured an axe, and turned towards the defendant with an imprecation and the statement that he would "fix him, etc." That defendant at once grabbed hold of the axe with deceased and both struggled violently for it. That defendant, being the younger man, and having on rubber-soled shoes, finally over-powered deceased, and got the axe away from him, and struck him with it in the groin, and then, as he lay on the deck or floor, nearly decapitated him by succeeding blows with the axe. Inferences were drawn from the testimony in argument that this could not have been true, but that, instead, defendant met deceased as he was coming down the stairway, and that, before deceased's head was below the deck, so that he could see defendant, the latter struck him in the groin with the axe and thus inflicted the mortal wound. It was in evidence by medical experts that the wound in the groin was first inflicted, and that it was fatal. This was determined from the lack of hemorrhage as a result of the wounds in the neck. There were many additional facts and circumstances, some of which may be gathered from the tenor of the court's instructions to the jury."

Instructions to the Petit Jury by Bernard S. Rodey, Judge[124]

"RODEY, Judge, omitting some of the formal parts, gave the following instructions to the jury:

The evidence in this cause all being in, and counsel having finished their arguments to you, it now becomes my duty to

---

[124] *Porto Rico Federal Reports*, Vol. IV, Honorable Henry F. Hord, Reporter, the Lawyer's Co-Operative Publishing company, Rochester, NY, 1909, pp 116-124

instruct you, as impartially as I may be capable of doing, as to what the law applicable to the case is, and what your duty in the premises is under the law. I might say here that you now have the greatest and most solemn duty connected with this case to perform; and it is assumed that, without prejudice or passion, and without fear or favor, you will proceed to do your duty as your lights give you to see the same, and in obedience to the law as given you in these instructions and the facts as you shall find them for yourselves; and that no occurrence at the trial between the court and counsel or in any other manner, not amounting to evidence in the case, will have any effect whatsoever upon you, either in your deliberations or in the returning of your verdict in the cause. Your consciences alone are burdened with the final duty of saying whether this defendant is guilty or not guilty under the proofs and the law of the case.

This is an indictment by the United States of America, charging the defendant, Alexander Dickson, with having, on the 20th day of February, A. D. 1908, in the bay of San Juan, Porto Rico, within the admiralty and maritime jurisdiction of the United States of America, and out of the jurisdiction of any particular state thereof, and within the jurisdiction of this court, in and on board of a certain vessel of the United States, to wit, the steamship Albarenda [sic], with force and arms, unlawfully, feloniously, and wilfully [sic] made an assault upon one Walter Weichert, with an axe, or some other sharp instrument, and then and there inflicting such wounds upon him that he died. The first count in the indictment charges the defendant with inflicting these wounds with an axe, and the second count charges him with inflicting them with some sharp instrument.

You are instructed that the venue is important in this case, and that this court has no jurisdiction to try this case unless you believe, from the evidence, that the acts charged did occur at the time and place stated in the indictment, or at such place some time or date within two years next previous to the return of the indictment.

The indictment is returned under § 5341 of the Revised Statute of the United States (U. S. Comp. Stat. 1901, p. 3628), which is as follows: "Every person who, within any of the places or upon any of the waters described in section fifty-three hundred and thirty-nine, unlawfully and wilfully, [sic] but without malice, strikes, stabs, wounds, or shoots at, or otherwise injures, another, of which striking, stabbing, wounding, shooting, or other injury such other person dies, either on land or sea, within or without the United States, is guilty of the crime of manslaughter."

The punishment for manslaughter is provided for by the act of March 3, 1875, chap. 138 (18 Stat. at L. 473, U. S. Comp. Stat. 1901, p. 3629), which reads as follows: "That whoever shall hereafter be convicted of the crime of manslaughter in any court of the United States, in any state or territory, including the District of Columbia, shall be imprisoned not exceeding ten years, and fined not exceeding one thousand dollars."

You will notice that the jury have nothing to do with the fixing of the punishment; they simply find the defendant guilty or not guilty of the crime charged, and the court itself, within the limits fixed by law, will impose the punishment or discharge the defendant, as he may be found guilty or not guilty by the jury. If he is found guilty, the court may impose any sentence it deems proper within the law, considering all the facts and circumstances of the case, but it must be both imprisonment and a fine ; but the imprisonment can be from one day to ten years, and the fine can be from 1 cent to $1,000.

You are instructed that, the grand jury having, in its wisdom, returned the indictment for manslaughter only, and not for murder, therefore the government is relieved from proving that the act was committed with malice, and you cannot find the defendant guilty of any higher crime than manslaughter ; but you are instructed that the fact that the grand jury did not indict for murder, but, instead, indicted for manslaughter only, is not evidence, as and of itself, that the defendant is guilty even of that crime, and you cannot so find him guilty unless the government has, on this trial, proved him to be guilty to your satisfaction as reasonable men, beyond a reasonable doubt.

You are instructed that the court has to go to the common law for a definition of manslaughter because there is no United States statute sufficiently defining it, and that it is the unlawful killing of a human being, without malice, expressed or implied.

A homicide is manslaughter when committed with the design to kill, under the influence of sudden and violent passion, caused by great provocation, which the law, in its tenderness to the infirmity of human nature, considers such a palliative as to rebut the presumption which would otherwise arise of malice, and make the crime murder. Under the wording of the statute as to this case, the killing must have been done unlawfully and willfully. "Unlawfully," as here used, means without legal excuse ; and "wilfully" [sic] means done wrongfully, with evil intent.

You are instructed that, under the indictment, the action of the defendant in this case is either manslaughter or justifiable homicide. To be justifiable homicide the defendant must have had good reason to believe, at the time he inflicted the wounds that caused the death, that the deceased was either about to take his life or to inflict great bodily injury upon him; and if you do not believe, beyond a reasonable doubt, that the defendant so believed or had any reasonable ground to so believe, then you should find the defendant guilty as charged in the indictment. If, on the contrary, you believe from the evidence that the defendant, at the time he inflicted the wounds which caused the death, upon the deceased, had good ground to believe that his own life was in immediate, imminent, and great danger, or that he was in danger of having inflicted upon him by the deceased great bodily injury, then you should find him not guilty, because his act would be in law justifiable homicide.

You are instructed that, while no man is obliged to submit to the wrongful infliction upon him by another of great bodily injury without resisting it if he can, still, no person can rightfully take the life of another when that other is not in a position to inflict great or grevious [sic] bodily injury upon him ; and if you believe, from the evidence in this case, beyond a reasonable doubt, that this defendant took the life of the deceased at a time when the deceased was not in a position to inflict great bodily injury upon him, and that the defendant could see and know, and did see and know, that the deceased was not in a position to inflict great bodily injury upon him, then you should find the defendant guilty as charged in the indictment.

If, on the other hand, you believe from the evidence, beyond a reasonable doubt, that, in this case, the deceased made, or was about to make, an unlawful assault upon the defendant, and first got hold of a deadly weapon which they both struggled for, then, if, in the struggle, the defendant got that deadly weapon away from the deceased, and, in the heat of passion, hit him such a blow with it as that it resulted in his death, the act would be justifiable homicide, and you should acquit the defendant.

You are instructed that every defendant is presumed by law to be innocent of the crime charged against him until the government has made out a case against him that satisfies you, as reasonable men, of his guilt beyond a reasonable doubt ; and this applies even though the defense is that the killing was done in self-defense. A reasonable doubt has been well defined to be a doubt of the defendant's guilt that remains in your minds as reasonable men, after a full, fair, and impartial consideration of all the facts and circumstances of the case, and not a mere possibility of the innocence of the defendant. If, after such a full, fair, and impartial consideration of all the facts and circumstances of this case, you have such an abiding doubt of the defendant's guilt, it is your duty to acquit him; and if, on the contrary, there remains no such reasonable doubt in your minds after such consideration, it is equally your duty to find the defendant guilty as charged in the indictment. You are instructed that the defendant need not have testified in this cause without he chose to do so, under our Constitution, and, had he not testified, you could not take the fact that he remained silent against him. On the other hand, neither can you take the fact that he has chosen to testify in his own behalf against him, because his evidence is entitled to the same weight that the evidence of any other witness is, save that you may, when considering the weight to be given to his evidence or that of any other witness in the case, consider his or their manner upon the stand, and the interest which he or they may have in the result of the case, and the probability or improbability of the truth of their stories to your minds as reasonable men. Under the law, the court is the judge of what the law is in this and nearly every other case ; and it is the sworn duty of the jury to take the law from the court ; but, as to the facts of the case, and the weight to be given to them, the jury are the sole judges, and their own recollection of what the testimony is must be taken in preference to that stated in the arguments of counsel on either side, or any statement that the court may make of it. In considering the testimony, if you believe that any witness has wilfully [sic] sworn falsely, you may disregard the whole or any portion of such witness's evidence unless the same shall be corroborated by other facts and circumstances of the case.

You are further instructed that, no matter what the feeling of other sailors or employees of the ship in question may have been toward the deceased, that fact can have no weight in justifying or excusing the taking of the life of the deceased, save in so far as the defendant's knowledge of the deceased's temper and disposition may have justified the belief of the defendant that his own life was in danger at the time he did the acts which the evidence may show you were done.

Two forms of verdict will be given you, one reading, "We, the jury, find the defendant guilty as charged in the indictment;" and the other, "We, the jury, find the defendant not guilty."

When you arrive at a verdict you will select the one of these forms that embodies it, and cause it to be signed by one of your number whom you will select as foreman for that purpose, and all of you will then call upon the marshal to bring you into court, so that you may return it. You may take to your room, where you go for your deliberations, the exhibits introduced in the case, if you choose, the indictment, and these instructions. The cause is with you." [125]

The Dickson trial was based on the definition of manslaughter as explained by the court stated that it, "... is the unlawful killing of a human being without malice, expressed or implied." "The killing of deceased by defendant in the heat of passion, with the same weapon with which deceased had just tried to kill defendant, would, under the law, be manslaughter or justifiable homicide, as the facts might warrant."[126]

Verdict

The court's journal, written in formal legal style, briefly described, Alexander Dickson's trial by jury on March 31, 1908.

---

[125] United States v. Alexander Dickson, *Porto Rico Federal Reports*, Honorable Henry F. Hord, Reporter, The Lawyers Co-Operative Publishing Company, Rochester, NY., 1909, pp. 116-124

[126] *Porto Rico Federal Reports*, Vol. IV, Honorable Henry F. Hord, Reporter, the Lawyer's Co-Operative Publishing company, Rochester, NY, 1909, pp 116-124

"In this cause again come the jury and after having been duly called are all found present. Again comes the defendant in his own proper person, in the custody of the Marshal, and come also his attorneys, W.H. Hawkins, Esq., and Joseph Anderson, Jr., Esq., and come also the United States by its attorney J.R.F. Savage, Esq., when the trial of the cause is proceeded with, and the jury having heard all of the witnesses, and seen and examined all of the exhibits and other proofs, and having heard arguments by the respective counsel, and having received the instructions of the Court, retire to consider of their verdict. And thereafter again come the jury and after having been again duly called and all found present, then and there in the presence of the defendant and his counsel, in open court, return the following verdict, that is to say: "We the jury, find the defendant not guilty." J.A. Canals, Foreman."[127]

Cause for an Additional Trial

The Sun, a New York City newspaper reported that, "It came out that in the course of the trial that he [Dickson] and other members of the crew had been treated with gross cruelty by Wichert [sic] and Capt. Worley."[128]

---

[127] U.S. vs. Alexander Dickson, pp. 525 - 526; Criminal Record; U.S. District Court for the District of Puerto Rico; Records of District Courts of the United States, Record Group 21; National Archives at New York City
[128] Abarenda Cruelty Inquiry, *The Sun*, New York, NY, May 09, 1908, p. 3

Master Worley's Trial

"From all accounts the U.S. collier Abarenda with a complement of merchant officers and crew, was a perfect "Hell ship," and frightful tales of the brutality of officers to the crew are told."[129]

The United States vs. George Worley
No. 408, Criminal

Judge of the District Court of the United States for Porto Rico
Bernard Shandon Rodey

United States Attorney
José R.F. Savage

Grand Jury Foreman
Nathanial A. Walcott

Clerk
John L. Gay

March 18, 1908 - Grand Jury Indictment filed. Capias ordered to issue.

---

[129] ABARENDA A "HELL SHIP" Quoted from *Army and Navy Journal*, republished in *The Pacific Commercial Advertiser*, Honolulu, Hawaii Territory, Tuesday, April 28, 1908, p. 7

From the Grand Jury indictment:

"UNITED STATES OF AMERICA,)
)
DISTRICT OF PORTO RICO.)

Indictment for:
Administering Corporal Punishment and Maltreating Seamen, R.S § 4611 and 5347

In the District Court of the United States in and for the District aforesaid, at the October Term thereof, A. D. 1907, The Grand Jurors of the United States, impaneled, sworn, and charged at the Term aforesaid, of the court aforesaid, on their oath present…"

(Complaint by Seaman T. Hunter Barnes)
"…that George Worley, on or about the 10th day of February, in the year 1908, on the high seas, within the admiralty and maritime jurisdiction of the United States of America and out of the jurisdiction of any particular state thereof, and within the jurisdiction of this court, in and on board of a certain vessel of the United States of America, to wit, the steamship called the "Abarenda", which said vessel was then and there owned by the said United States of America,"

"with force and arms, in and upon T.H. Barnes did make an assault, and then and there, he, the said George Worley with his hand, in and upon the said T.H. Barnes did administer corporal punishment, by striking him, the said T. H. Barnes;"

"with force and arms, in and upon T.H. Barnes did make an assault, and him the said T.H. Barnes then and there did unlawfully and willfully beat and ill-treat, without justifiable cause; he the said George Worley being then and there the master of said vessel," "and the said T.H. Barnes being then and there a member of and one of the crew of the said vessel, contrary to the form of the statute in such case made and provided, and against the peace and dignity of the United States."[130]

Complaint by Seaman Louis E. Chinal

"...that George Worley, on or about the 1st day of January, in the year 1908, on the high seas, within the admiralty and maritime jurisdiction of the United States of America and out of the jurisdiction of any particular state thereof, and within the jurisdiction of this court, in and on board of a certain vessel of the United States of America, to wit, the steamship called the "Abarenda", which said vessel was then and there owned by the said United States of America,"

"with force and arms, in and upon Louis E. Chinal did make an assault, and him the said Louis E. Chinal then and there did unlawfully and willfully beat and ill-treat, without justifiable cause;"

"with force and arms, and upon Louis E. Chinal did make an assault, and then and there, he, the said George Worley with his hand, in and upon the said Louis E. Chinal did administer corporal punishment, by striking him, the said Louis E. Chinal;"

"the said George Worley being then and there the master of said vessel, and the said Louis E. Chinal being then and there a member of and one of the crew of the said vessel, contrary to the

---

[130] Case File 408; Criminal Case Files; U.S. District Court for the District of Puerto Rico; Records of District Courts of the United States, Record Group 21; National Archives at New York City

form of the statute in such case made and provided, and against the peace and dignity of the United States."[131]

Complaint by Seaman Patrick Gallagher

"…that the said George Worley, on or about the 10th day of February, in the year 1908, in the bay of Rio [de] Janeiro, Brazil, and within the admiralty and maritime jurisdiction of the United States of America and out of the jurisdiction of any particular state thereof, and within the jurisdiction of this court, in and on board of a certain vessel, to wit, the steamship called the "Abarenda", which said vessel was then and there owned by the United States of America, with force and arms, in and upon Patrick Gallagher, did make an assault, and in and upon him, the said Patrick Gallagher, without justifiable cause, did then and there inflict a certain cruel and unusual punishment, in that he, the said George Worley did cause the said Patrick Gallagher to be hung up in irons; he, the said George Worley being, then and there, the master of the said vessel; and the said Patrick Gallagher being one of the crew of the said vessel; contrary to the form of the statute in such case made and provided, and against the peace and dignity of the United States."[132]

Complaint by Seaman George Marsden

"…that the said George Worley, on or about the 10th day of February, in the year 1908, in the bay of Rio Janeiro, Brazil, and

---

[131] Case File 408; Criminal Case Files; U.S. District Court for the District of Puerto Rico; Records of District Courts of the United States, Record Group 21; National Archives at New York City

[132] Case File 408; Criminal Case Files; U.S. District Court for the District of Puerto Rico; Records of District Courts of the United States, Record Group 21; National Archives at New York City

within the admiralty and maritime jurisdiction of the United States of America and out of the jurisdiction of any particular state thereof, and within the jurisdiction of this court, in and on board of a certain American vessel, to wit, the steamship called the "Abarenda", which said vessel was then and there owned by the United States of America, with force and arms, in and upon George Marsden, did make an assault, and in and upon him, the said George Marsden, without justifiable cause, did then and there inflict a certain cruel and unusual punishment, in that he, the said George Worley did cause the said George Marsden to be hung up in irons; he, the said George Worley being, then and there, the master of the said vessel; and the said George Marsden being one of the crew of the said vessel; contrary to the form of the statute in such case made and provided, and against the peace and dignity of the United States."[133]

"…in violation of Sections 4611 and 5347 R.S.U.S., (Revised Statutes of the United States) and charging that in the District Court in and for the District of Porto Rico on the 18th day of March, 1908, the grand jury of the United States returned an indictment against the said George Worley for the offenses aforesaid…"[134]

Section 4611, Revised Statutes of the United States [As amended 1898.]: "[Corporal punishment prohibited: penalty.] Flogging and all other forms of corporal punishment are hereby prohibited on board any vessel, and no form of corporal punishment on board any vessel shall be deemed justifiable, and any master or other officer thereof who shall violate the aforesaid provisions of this

---

[133] Case File 408; Criminal Case Files; U.S. District Court for the District of Puerto Rico; Records of District Courts of the United States, Record Group 21; National Archives at New York City

[134] Case File 408; Criminal Case Files; U.S. District Court for the District of Puerto Rico; Records of District Courts of the United States, Record Group 21; National Archives at New York City

section or either thereof shall be deemed guilty of a misdemeanor, punishable by imprisonment not less than three months or more than two years. Whenever any officer other than the master of such vessel shall violate any provision of this section, it shall be the duty of such master to surrender such officer to the proper authorities as soon as practicable. Any failure upon the part of such master to comply herewith, which failure shall result in the escape of such officer, shall render said master liable in damages to the person illegally punished by such officer."[135]

Section 5347, Revised Statutes of the United States [As amended 1897.]: "Maltreatment of crew by officers of vessels. Every master or other officer of an American vessel on the high seas or any other waters within the admiralty and maritime jurisdiction of the United States, who, without justifiable cause, beats, wounds, or imprisons and of the crew of such vessel or withholds from them suitable food and nourishment, shall be punished by a fine of not more than one thousand dollars, or by imprisonment not more than five years, or by both."[136]

March 19, 1908 – "Capias issued."

March 24, 1908 - Capias filed. Defendant not found. H.S. Hubbard, U.S. Marshal was unable to find the defendant George Worley.[137]

March 31, 1908 – "A United States marshal boarded the Abarenda in the (Brooklyn, New York) Navy Yard to arrest the Captain, who has been declared a fugitive from justice and to cause his return to San Juan to stand trial, but he was advised that the man he was after had left the yard and the city and was undoubtedly on

---

[135] *Compiled Statues of the United States 1901*, Volume 3, Compiled by John A. Mallory, West Publishing Co., St. Paul, MN, 1902, p. 3120
[136] *Compiled Statues of the United States 1901*, Compiled by John A. Mallory, Volume 1, West Publishing Co., St. Paul, MN, 1902, p. 3631
[137] Case File 408; Criminal Case Files; U.S. District Court for the District of Puerto Rico; Records of District Courts of the United States, Record Group 21; National Archives at New York City

his way to Bremerton, Wash., where he maintains a home for his wife and child."[138] The ship arrived at the Navy Yard on March 10th.[139] "A few days later Worley asked for, and was granted, leave of absence for 90 days on the ground that he was physically incapacitated and would have to undergo an operation."[140]

April 1, 1908 - Motion filed by United States Attorney José R.F. Savage, "For order for appearance bond of T.H. Barnes, Louis E. Chinal, George Marsden, Patrick Gallagher and John Goodro necessary witnesses in above-entitled cause. On account of inability to give bond, the Court orders detention of Barnes, Chinal, Marsden, Gallagher and Goodro for three days from this date."[141]

April 4, 1908 - United States Attorney, "moves that Barnes, Chinal, Marsden, Gallagher, and Goodro be detained to and including the 6th inst., and it is so ordered."[142]

April 6, 1908 – "On motion of U.S. Atty., Barnes, Chinal, Marsden, Gallagher, and Goodro are ordered detained until and including April 10th." Elmer E. Todd, U.S. Attorney for the Western District of Washington presented an affidavit to James

---

[138] After Navy Captain, *Baltimore American*, Baltimore, MD, April 1, 1908, p. 1
[139] Log of the United States Naval Auxiliary *Abarenda*, Record Group 24; National Archives Bldg., Washington, DC
[140] After Navy Captain, *Baltimore American*, Baltimore, MD, April 1, 1908, p. 1
[141] Case File 408; Criminal Case Files; U.S. District Court for the District of Puerto Rico; Records of District Courts of the United States, Record Group 21; National Archives at New York City
[142] Case File 408; Criminal Case Files; U.S. District Court for the District of Puerto Rico; Records of District Courts of the United States, Record Group 21; National Archives at New York City

Kiefer, U. S. Commissioner, charging that George Worley violated Sections 4611 and 5347 R.S.U.S."[143]

April 7, 1908 – Master George W. Worley had been "brought into the court by Fred M. Lathe, Deputy United States Marshal…" The warrant was returned endorsed: "Received this warrant on the 6th day of April 1908, at Seattle Washington, and executed the same by arresting the within named George Worley at Seattle, Washington on the 7th day of April, 1908, and have his body now in court as within I am commanded. C.B. Hopkins, U.S. Marshal." "The prisoner made a statement on his own behalf and thereupon the Commissioner finds that the prisoner is the person named in said indictment…" James Kiefer, U. S. Commissioner for the Western District of Washington, received from George Worley, $500.00 "deposited as security in lieu of bail bond for his appearance before the United States District court in and for the District of Porto Rico…" The Commissioner's fee was $8.25.[144]

April 10, 1908 – "Motion by U.S. Atty. for further detention of Barnes, Chinal, Marsden, Gallagher and Goodro considered and denied, said witnesses to be released on personal recognizance, to which U.S. Atty. excepts."[145]

April 16, 1908 – "On motion of U.S. Atty. it is ordered that Barnes, Gallagher and. Marsden be committed to the custody of the U.S. Marshal until the trial of this cause is finished."[146]

---

[143] Case File 408; Criminal Case Files; U.S. District Court for the District of Puerto Rico; Records of District Courts of the United States, Record Group 21; National Archives at New York City

[144] Case File 408; Criminal Case Files; U.S. District Court for the District of Puerto Rico; Records of District Courts of the United States, Record Group 21; National Archives at New York City

[145] Case File 408; Criminal Case Files; U.S. District Court for the District of Puerto Rico; Records of District Courts of the United States, Record Group 21; National Archives at New York City

[146] Case File 408; Criminal Case Files; U.S. District Court for the District of Puerto Rico; Records of District Courts of the United States, Record Group 21; National Archives at New York City

April 20, 1908 – "On motion of U.S. Atty. it is ordered that Louis E. Chinal be committed to the custody Of the U.S. Marshal until the trial of this cause is finished."[147]

April 22, 1908 – "ABARENDA sailed twenty-first Bradford San Juan 3542 tons Pocahontas. Invoice three twenty."[148]

April 23, 1908 – "Received transcript of proceedings had in case of U.S. vs. George Worley before James Kiefer, U.S. Commissioner for the Western District of Washington, together with duplicate receipt for $500 deposited as security in lieu of bail bond for Worley's appearance before the U.S. Dist. Court for P.R., and draft of The Scandinavian American Bank, Seattle, Wash., on the Seaboard National Bank, New York, for $500.00 payable to Geo. Worley, indorsed by Worley to James Kiefer, and indorsed by James Kiefer to John L. Gay, Clerk U.S. Dist. Court for P.R."[149]

April 29, 1908 – A telegram from Rear Admiral John E. Pillsbury, Chief, Bureau of Navigation, to the San Juan Naval Station: "Discharge Abarenda[.] Do not detain[.]"[150]

---

[147] Case File 408; Criminal Case Files; U.S. District Court for the District of Puerto Rico; Records of District Courts of the United States, Record Group 21; National Archives at New York City

[148] Telegram (175,249 FAW-H) from Rear Admiral William C. Cowles, Chief, Bureau of Equipment, that duplicated original message sent the same day from San Juan Naval Station to Washington, DC. San Juan Naval Station Letters Received by Commandant, Entry 732, Records of Naval Station San Juan, P.R., Naval Districts and Shore Establishments, Record Group 181; National Archives and Records Administration - Northeast Region (New York City).

[149] Case File 408; Criminal Case Files; U.S. District Court for the District of Puerto Rico; Records of District Courts of the United States, Record Group 21; National Archives at New York City.

[150] Telegram (handwritten on West India and Panama Telegraph Company, Limited form) prior to typing at receiving end) from Rear Admiral John E. Pillsbury, Chief, Bureau of Navigation, Washington, DC to the San Juan Naval Station, April 9, 1908, San Juan Naval Station Letters Received by Commandant, Entry 732, Records of Naval Station San Juan, P.R., Naval Districts and Shore

May 4, 1908 - Acting Navy Secretary Newberry announced that a court of inquiry would be appointed at Norfolk, Virginia to examine the charges of cruel treatment, by seventeen men of the *Abarenda*, against their former commander, Master Worley.[151] A partially coded telegram was sent by Rear Admiral John E. Pillsbury, Chief, Bureau of Navigation, to the San Juan Naval Station: "Direct abarenda proceed Norfolk infilmed cortinulis"[152] The term: "infilmed" decoded, "as soon as they can"; "cortinulis" decoded, "when discharged". The fully decoded message: Direct Abarenda proceed Norfolk as soon as they can when discharged.[153]

May 5, 1908 - Acting Navy Secretary Newberry to the San Juan Naval Station: "Send all of Abarenda[']s old crew north with her[.] If any have been discharged direct that they be reshipped[.] Consult with district attorney[.]"[154]

May 6, 1908 - U.S. District Court for the District of Puerto Rico ordered that the "U.S. Marshal turn Gallagher, Marsden, Barnes, and Chinal over to Commandant of Naval Station, San Juan, P.R.,

---

Establishments, Record Group 181; National Archives and Records Administration - Northeast Region (New York City).
[151] Court of Inquiry on Collier Cruelty, *The Boston Journal*, Boston, MA, May 5, 1908, p. 5
[152] Telegram (handwritten on West India and Panama Telegraph Company, Limited form) prior to typing at receiving end) from Rear Admiral John E. Pillsbury, Chief, Bureau of Navigation, Washington, DC to the San Juan Naval Station, May 4, 1908, San Juan Naval Station Letters Received by Commandant, Entry 732, Records of Naval Station San Juan, P.R., Naval Districts and Shore Establishments, Record Group 181; National Archives and Records Administration - Northeast Region, New York City
[153] Terms: "infilmed", "cortinulis", *Western Union Telegraphic Code*, Universal Edition, Compiled and Published by International Cable Directory Company, New York, NY, 1903, pp. 119, 127
[154] Telegram (handwritten on West India and Panama Telegraph Company, Limited form) prior to typing at receiving end) from Acting Navy Secretary Newberry, Washington, DC to the San Juan Naval Station, May 5, 1908, San Juan Naval Station Letters Received by Commandant, Entry 732, Records of Naval Station San Juan, P.R., Naval Districts and Shore Establishments, Record Group 181; National Archives and Records Administration - Northeast Region, New York City

in accordance with orders received by U.S. Atty. from the Atty. Gen'l of the U.S."[155]

May 7, 1908 – U.S. Marshal ordered to take into custody Gallagher, Marsden, Barnes, and Chinal.[156] Rear Admiral John E. Pillsbury, Chief, Bureau of Navigation, to the San Juan Naval Station: "Direct ABARENDA proceed Bradford [RI] instead Norfolk."[157]

May 8, 1908 - San Juan, Porto Rico, "The crew of the United States collier Abarenda refuse to go to Norfolk and are again in the custody of the Federal authorities pending the receipt of instructions from Washington. Alexander Dickson, a carpenter on the collier, killed Chief Officer Weichert at San Juan, February 20. He was indicted for manslaughter, tried here and acquitted. At the same time the grand jury indicted Captain Worley, of the collier, for cruelty, and he is now being tried by a naval court at Norfolk. The crew of Abarenda which has been held here since April are wanted as witnesses against the captain and the Department of Justice ordered them to sail on the collier assuming that they were still enlisted men. They base their refusal to go on the allegation that they were discharged when the trial occurred."[158]

---

[155] Case File 408; Criminal Case Files; U.S. District Court for the District of Puerto Rico; Records of District Courts of the United States, Record Group 21; National Archives at New York City

[156] Case File 408; Criminal Case Files; U.S. District Court for the District of Puerto Rico; Records of District Courts of the United States, Record Group 21; National Archives at New York City

[157] Telegram (DFS-JTG) from Rear Admiral John E. Pillsbury, Chief, Bureau of Navigation, Washington, DC to San Juan Naval Station, May 7, 1908, San Juan Naval Station Letters Received by Commandant, Entry 732, Records of Naval Station San Juan, P.R., Naval Districts and Shore Establishments, Record Group 181; National Archives and Records Administration - Northeast Region, New York City

[158] Collier Crew Mutini [sic], Refuses to Sail on Ground it Has Been Discharged, *The Patriot*, Harrisburg, PA, May 9, 1908, p. 16

May 9, 1908 - U.S. District Court ordered U.S. Marshal to release Gallagher, Marsden, Barnes, and Chinal.[159]

June 13, 1908 - Washington, D.C. "The naval board of which Captain Berry was chairman, has reported that the charges of cruelty preferred against Captain George Worley, merchant master of the naval collier Abarenda, by members of the crew have not been sustained by the evidence. No further action will be taken by the department."[160]

October 26, 1908 - "U.S. Atty. moves to dismiss case, and it is so ordered. Draft which was held in place of bond to be returned to defendant."[161]

---

[159] Case File 408; Criminal Case Files; U.S. District Court for the District of Puerto Rico; Records of District Courts of the United States, Record Group 21; National Archives at New York City

[160] Charges Not Sustained, *The Times Dispatch,* Richmond, VA, June 14, 1908, p. 6D

[161] The United States vs. George Worley, Docket 2, p. 6; Criminal Dockets; U.S. District Court for the District of Puerto Rico; Records of District Courts of the United States, Record Group 21; National Archives at New York City

Irons

The use of "irons" and "double irons" in conjunction with disciplinary confinement in the *Abarenda's* brig was not uncommon. The ship's 1907 and 1908 logbooks contain many instances of enlisted men who were placed in irons or double irons for various infractions.

During the time of First Officer Weichert's service on the collier, the *Abarenda* was manned by civilians and operated under the Naval Auxiliary Service which had its own published regulations. The rules pertaining to the use of irons were not explicit, in fact, the word "irons" does not appear anywhere in the 1907 edition of the *Regulations for the Naval Auxiliary Service* in effect April 1, 1907 - April 30, 1908:

"CHAPTER IV.
PUNISHMENTS.

49. Punishments shall be in strict conformity with law and in accordance with the usages of the sea service, and will follow the offense as promptly as circumstances will permit.[162]

50. The master shall not impose upon persons under his command any other punishment than the following:

(a) Upon officers: Private reprimand, suspension from duty, or confinement for a period not longer than ten days.

(b) Upon members of the crew: No others than those authorized by the navigation laws of the United States, and all

---

[162] Chapter IV, "Punishments", *Regulations for the Naval Auxiliary Service*, Bureau of Navigation, Department of the Navy, 1907 (in effect April 1, 1907 - April 30, 1908) Government Printing Office, Washington, DC, p. 15

punishments so inflicted must be strictly in accordance with those laws.

51. All punishments inflicted by the master, except reprimands, shall be fully entered in the ship's log. This entry must include the rank or rating of the offender, the date and nature of the offense, and the kind and degree of punishment. The termination of the punishment shall be noted also."[163]

The legality of the use of irons was documented in the U.S. Navy's 1905 regulations: "Confinement in double irons is a severe punishment, and, as a rule, should not be resorted to, at least not for any considerable period, except where the offense has been grave or the offender has given indications of being incorrigible after the infliction of milder punishment."[164]

The March 13, 1908 edition of the *Los Angeles Herald* included the syndicated *Daily Naval Report* from Washington, D.C. In its *Navy Notes* section was an update on the upcoming trial of Alexander "Dickson who is accused of the murder of Weichert…" That was immediately followed by, "Senator Nelson has offered an amendment to the naval bill by which the use of irons, single or double, upon navy prisoners is prohibited."[165]

Given the publication's timing and consecutive placement of the two news pieces, it would seem reasonable that they represented a cause and effect. The killing of First Officer Weichert which followed his assailant's release from punitive confinement "for deliberately destroying ship's property and using

---

[163] Chapter IV, "Punishments", *Regulations for the Naval Auxiliary Service*, Bureau of Navigation, Department of the Navy, 1907 (in effect April 1, 1907 - April 30, 1908) Government Printing Office, Washington, DC, p. 15
[164] *Regulations for the Government of the Navy of the United States*, Chapter XLI, Summary Court Martial, Government Printing Office, Washington, DC, 1905, p. 472
[165] Daily Naval Report, *Los Angeles Herald*, Los Angeles, CA, March 13, 1908, p. 4

threatening language toward first officer."[166] That comparison does not fit since Alexander Dickson had not been placed in irons for those offenses.

The next possible connection could be the indictment and trial of Master George Worley, for causing two of his men on the *Abarenda* to be "hung in irons",[167] among other charges of cruelty. His indictment occurred after the publication of the article, although it's possible that rumors may have found their way to the halls of Congress prior to any legislative action.

Senator Knute Nelson, of Minnesota, submitted an amendment to the naval appropriation bill that would abolish the "use of irons, single or double, as a form of punishment in the Navy". His amendment actually originated with a letter sent to the Senator, early in March 1908, by a constituent on behalf of her sister, Emma P. Olberg of La Crosse, Wisconsin. In 1906, Mrs. Olberg traveled to Boston, Massachusetts to visit her enlisted son who's ship was in port. Because of her interest in the welfare of the "blue jackets" she also visited the naval hospitals in the area. She already believed that irons should be abolished in the navy, but took up the cause upon seeing hospitalized sailors with their feet shackled to their cots. Her east coast travels took her to the Brooklyn Navy Yard where she witnessed "men shacked hands and feet hobbling over the rough cobblestones..."[168]

---

[166] Log of the United States Naval Auxiliary Abarenda, Record Group 24; National Archives Bldg., Washington, DC

[167] Case File 408; Criminal Case Files; U.S. District Court for the District of Puerto Rico; Records of
District Courts of the United States, Record Group 21; National Archives at New York City.

[168] *Congressional Record,* 60th Congress, 1st Session, Senate, Government Printing Office, Washington, DC, April 23, 1908, pp. 5117-5118

The amendment was included in the appropriations bill with one proviso: "except for the purposes of safe custody or when part of the sentence imposed by a general court-martial."

"ACT MAY 13, 1908, c. 166. H. R. 20471.] Use of irons as punishment restricted. That the use of irons, single or double, as a form of punishment in the Navy of the United States is hereby abolished, except for the purposes of safe custody or when part of the sentence imposed by a general court-martial. (Act May 13, 1908, c. 166, 35 Stat. 132. This is a provision of the Navy appropriation act for the fiscal year ending June 30, 1909, cited above.)"[169]

The prohibition on the use of irons as a form of punishment was incorporated into the 1909 edition of *Regulations for the Government of the Navy of the United States*; however, no changes were made to the *Regulations for the Naval Auxiliary Service*. George W. Worley resumed his use of single irons from 1911 to 1913 on the collier *Cyclops*.

---

[169] Compiled Statutes of the United States Supplement -1911, West Publishing, St. Paul, MN, 1912, p. 417

Weichert in the Spanish American War

Two years prior to the commencement of his sea service, Walter R. Weichert answered his country's call. On June 26, 1898, two months after the United States declared war against Spain, twenty six year old Walter Weichert enlisted in the U.S. Army at Siboney, Cuba. A former sailor, Weichert joined Company D, 9th Infantry Regiment as a Private for a three year enlistment. The character of the 5'8" soldier was noted as "excellent" in his enlistment record.[170] "Records of Physical Examination at Enlistment show: "Slight rupture. Defective vision due to astigmatism."[171]

From the official "report of the part taken by Company D, Ninth United States Infantry, in the battle of Fort San Juan, Cuba, July 1, 1898:" "The company came under fire" and "moved forward in single file…" They "underwent a lively fire" as they "marched down the narrow passage between thick bushes until" they "arrived at the crossing of the San Juan River," where they "waded the stream under a shower of bullets." To their front, "was the blockhouse, south of which, along the crest and clearly outlined against the sky, was a swarm of Spaniards. From these latter and from troops in the trenches around the blockhouse the fire was furious." The company moved through the creek in water which was up to their waists. "Treetop entanglements" in their front caused them to "cut through the barbed-wire fence on the

---

[170] Enlistment record, Walter R. Weichert, Albany, New York; Abstracts of Spanish-American War Military and Naval Service Records, 1898-1902; Series Number: B0809

[171] Report from F.C. Ainsworth, The Adjutant General. U.S. Army to the Commissioner of Pensions, April 6, 1908, Pension file no. 925721, Record Group 15; National Archives Bldg., Washington, DC

bank", where they "quickly got into a line of skirmishers and moved forward to the elevated position..." They "delivered several volleys on retiring Spaniards." Despite bullets that whistled over them, they held their position "as directed, during the hot afternoon. In the evening, with bayonets as picks and the hands as shovels, began the hasty intrenchments [sic]..." "The march down that valley of death and subsequent trying service has demonstrated that these are brave men." "...noncommissioned officers and privates of the company performed their duties well."[172]

"W. R. Weichert, of New York, a member of the Ninth infantry, was one of the fifteen men who captured the blockhouse at El Caney, occupied by thirty-five Spaniards, by entering through the roof." Weichert recalled, "It was certain death, we thought, but not a man flinched," he said. "The Spaniards had been shooting us through the holes in the blockhouse, and we could not penetrate their heavy timbers. We were ordered to the roof, nineteen of us. The first four jumped in and were as quickly slaughtered, and then we all dropped in at one time, and for twenty minutes the fighting was most desperate." "I engaged a Spaniard in a hand-to-hand bout, and was wounded in the arm. I wrenched his pistol from his hand and shot him dead." "Here is a souvenir," he added, displaying a Madrid-made revolver. "Every one of the thirty-five Spaniards was killed; of the original nineteen Americans only the first four were killed. This attack was made on July 1st."[173]

---

[172] Report by John M. Sigworth, First Lieutenant, Company D, Ninth United States Infantry, on the battle of Fort San Juan, Cuba, Annual Report of the Major General Commanding the Army to the Secretary of War, Government Printing Office, Washington, DC, 1898, p. 447

[173] Stories of the Regulars/A Fight to the Death, Chapter 5, *The Story of Our Wonderful Victories*, American Book and Bible House, Philadelphia, PA, 1899, p. 205

Private Weichert was shot in the arm by a bullet at San Juan Hill, Santiago, Cuba July 1, 1898.[174] He had actually been shot three times and was left for dead on the field until a Red Cross surgeon found him and saved his life[175] in the division hospital.[176] Weichert was discharged a month before the Treaty of Paris was signed which ended the war with Spain.[177]

Ten years later, Adjutant General, F.C. Ainsworth, U.S. Army, responded to an inquiry from the Commissioner of Pensions. He reported that Private Walter R. Weichert had been, "Wounded in action July 1, 1898 at the Battle of San Juan Hill, Cuba." "The medical records show him treated as follows: July - 1898, Gunshot wound right arm, in the line of duty; July 3 + 4, 1898, undetermined; July 11 to Aug. 4, 1898, Gunshot wound left arm. Hernia on both sides, in line of duty. Furloughed Aug. 4 to Oct. 3, 1898; Aug. 16 to 22, 1898. Adinitis [sic] inguinal glands both sides, non-veneral, and muscular rheumatism sub-acute, muscles of lumbar region, in line of duty. No additional record of disability found." He was honorably discharged on November 8, 1898.[178]

---

[174] Returns from Regular Army Infantry Regiments, June 1821–December 1916. NARA microfilm publication M665, roll 106 Records of the Adjutant General's Office, 1780's–1917, Record Group 94. National Archives and Records Administration, Washington, DC

[175] Weichart [sic] Wedded Here, *The Daily Picayune*, New Orleans, LA, March 8, 1908, p. 4

[176] Returns from Regular Army Infantry Regiments, June 1821–December 1916. NARA microfilm publication M665, roll 106 Records of the Adjutant General's Office, 1780's–1917, Record Group 94. National Archives and Records Administration, Washington, DC

[177] Enlistment record, Walter R. Weichert, Albany, New York; Abstracts of Spanish-American War Military and Naval Service Records, 1898-1902; Series Number: B0809

[178] Report from F.C. Ainsworth, The Adjutant General. U.S. Army to the Commissioner of Pensions, April 6, 1908, Pension file no. 925721, Record Group 15; National Archives Bldg., Washington, DC

"Co. D, 9th U.S. Infantry was stationed in the United States from April 21, 1898 to June 13, 1898, in Cuba from June 14, 1898 to August 14, 1898, and in the United States from August 15, 1898 to March 27, 1899."[179]

---

[179] Document prepared by S. G. Rogers, Chief of Army and Navy Division, Bureau of Pensions, based upon, "Circular showing the Distribution of Troops of the Line of the United States Army, January 1, 1866 to June 30, 1909" Compiled and Issued by the Adjutant General's Office, War Department

Walter Robert Weichert
First Officer, U.S.A.S. *Abarenda*

The Daily Picayune
New Orleans, Louisiana, March 8, 1908

Viola Ruth (nee Patterson) Weichert / Rampfeil
1964 Photograph
Courtesy, Lucille Weichert Croscup

Church of St. John the Baptist
Dryades Street, New Orleans, Louisiana
Courtesy of the Collections of the Louisiana State Museum

Helena Weichert (daughter of Walter and Viola Weichert)
from *"Blanco y Negro"* Newspaper Advertisement
La Prensa, San Antonio, TX, March 3, 1927

Viola Weichert (daughter of Walter and Viola Weichert)
from *Black and White Cold Cream* Newspaper Advertisement
Joplin Globe, Joplin, MO, March 15, 1927.

Robert L. Weichert
Son of Walter and Viola Weichert with
Infant Lucille Weichert
1941 Photograph, Courtesy, Lucille Weichert Croscup

Viola R. (nee Weichert) Ward
Daughter of Walter and Viola Weichert
1964 Photograph
Courtesy, Lucille Weichert Croscup

Robert L. Weichert & Eleanor (nee Bergeron) Weichert
1964 Photograph
Courtesy, Lucille Weichert Croscup

Lucille Weichert
Granddaughter of Walter Robert Weichert
1961 Photograph
Courtesy, Lucille Weichert Croscup

Grave Marker of Walter R. Weichert
Puerto Rico National Cemetery, Bayamon, P.R.
Section C, Grave 544
Author's 2013 photograph

Abarenda
1898 Photograph
Refitting as Collier for United States Navy
Naval History and Heritage Command

Collier Abarenda
1907 Photograph
Naval History and Heritage Command

under the command of _Geo. Horley Master_, U.S. Navy,
Thursday February 20th 1908

RECORD OF THE MISCELLANEOUS EVENTS OF THE DAY

Mid — 4
    Clear blue sky and light breeze.

4 — 8
    Cloudy and calm.

8 — Merid
    Partly cloudy. Fresh breeze.

Merid — 4
Between 12 and 1.30 p.m. First Officer H. R. Weichert was killed with an axe in the hands of Chas. Dixon, ships carpenter. Dixon immediately gave himself up to the Third Officer saying he had killed the First Officer and handing over the axe with which it was done. Dixon was taken in charge by marines from the Naval Station.
About 2.30 p.m. Board of Inquiry met aboard. The sitting of Council J. G. Bell, U.S. Navy, retired, P.A. Surgeon H.R. Webb, U.S.N., 1st Lieut. J.T. Halford, U.S. Marine Corps, members, and Chief Bos'n G. Duerendorf, U.S.N., recorder. Board of Inquiry adjourned at 4-45 having completed their labors.
The body of First Officer H. R. Weichert was taken charge of by Surgeon H. R. Webb U.S.N. and removed to the dispensary of the Naval Station to be prepared for interment. Colors set at half mast during the afternoon.
No work done by coal gang during the afternoon.
Crew engaged in painting ships sides.
Lights and pumps attended to.
Gear turnbuckles on watch.

12.50 Carpenter Dixon delibertely disobeying 1st Officer's orders sent to be refused to Norfolk Navy Yard

1.30 p.m. Seaman Gallagher returned aboard, 5.30 am over leave.

4 — Partly cloudy. Fresh breeze.

4 — 8
    Clear and calm.

8 — Mid
    Cloudy and calm.

Examined and found to be correct.
                                        Geo. Horley
                                             Navigator.

**First Officer Weichert's Murder documented in the
Log Book of the United States Naval Auxiliary *Abarenda***
February 20, 1908
RG 24, National Archives and Records Administration

NAVAL OFFICER SLAIN WITH AX

San Juan, Porto Rico, Feb. 21.—George Dixon, a carpenter on the American collier Abarenda, killed Walter Weichert, chief officer of the collier, today on board the vessel. Dixon swung at Weichert with an axe and completely severed his head. The attack was made just as Weichert was walking away from the carpenter's bench, where he had been talking with Dixon. Weichert recently had Dixon placed in irons on account of disobedience of orders, and this probably was the motive for the crime.

RECEIVED
MAR 26 1908

No............ 3rd Endorsement.

U. S. S. ABARENDA.

Navy Yard, Brooklyn, N. Y.
March 26, 1908.

SUBJECT:

Bureau of pensions: Requests descriptive list and history of service, and circumstances surrounding the murder of Walter R. Weichert, chief Officer, killed February 20, 1908. at San Juan, P. R.

---

1. Respectfully returned to the Supervisor Naval Auxiliaries, with the following information.

2. W. R. Weichert, served on the U. S. S. ABARENDA, as Chief Officer under my command from the 1st December 1907., to the 20th, February 1908, when he was cruelly murdered by Aleck Dickson, a carpenter with an axe, while said officer was intending to perform ship's duties. The murder took place at about noon, while the ship was alongside the Navy Yard, receiving bun-

ker coal. I was on shore when the murder occurred, therefore cannot give but a meagre description of what took place, only that I was informed that the carpenter had cut the Chief officer's head off with an axe.

3. During my acquaintance with Chief Officer Weichert, I found him to be an honest willing and able Officer, and well spoken of by all the Masters under whom he has served.

Geo. Worley
Master, N.A.S.

P.S. *[handwritten postscript, illegible]*

Geo. Worley

(continuation)
Master George Worley's response to an inquiry from the Supervisor of Naval Auxiliaries March 26, 1908
Pension file no. 925721, Walter R. Weichert, RG 15
National Archives and Records Administration

MARSHAL IS UNSUCCESSFUL.

Attempt Is Made to Arrest Captain George Worley at the New York Navy Yard.

New York, March 31.—It was learned today that an unsuccessful attempt was made by a United States Marshal yesterday at the New York Navy Yard to take into custody Capt. George Worley, formerly commander of the auxiliary United States naval vessel Abarenda, who was indicted by a Grand Jury at San Juan on a charge of treating his crew in an inhuman manner.

Capt. Worley is on leave of absence and is said to be on his way to his home in Brematore, Wash.

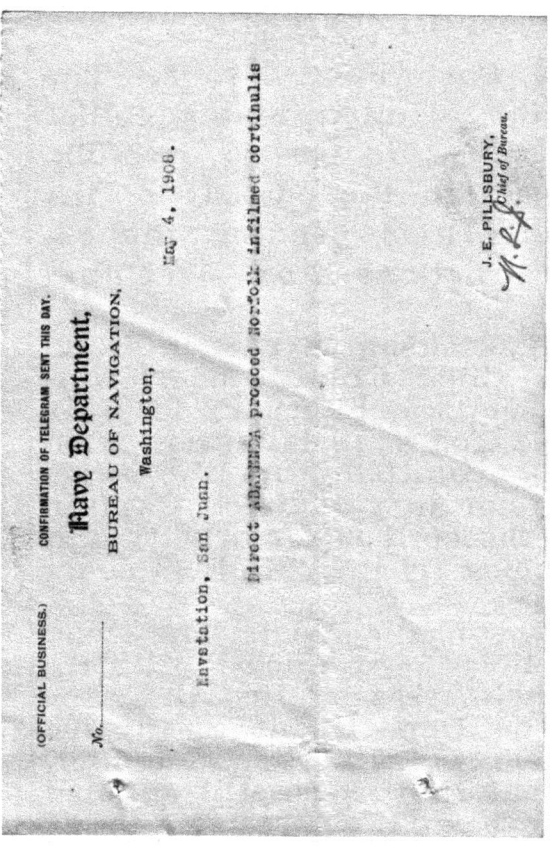

Telegram "infilmed cortinulis" May 4, 1908
From Rear Admiral John E. Pillsbury to San Juan Naval Station
Records of Naval Station San Juan, P.R.,
RG 181, National Archives and Records Administration,

COLLIER CREW MUTINI

Refuses to Sail On Ground It Has Been Discharged.

San Juan, Porto Rico. May 8.—The crew of the United States collier Abarenda refuse to go to Norfolk, and are again in the custody of the Federal authorities pending the receipt of instructions from Washington.

Alexander Dickson, a carpenter on the collier, killed Chief Officer Weichert at San Juan, February 20. He was indicted for manslaughter, tried here and acquitted. At the same time the grand jury indicted Captain Worley, of the collier, for cruelty and he is now being tried by a naval court at Norfolk.

The crew of the Abarenda, who have been held here since April, are wanted as witnesses against the captain, and the Department of Justice ordered them to sail on the collier, assuming that they were still enlisted men. They base their refusal to go on the allegation that they were discharged when the trial occurred.

Bernard Shandon Rodey
Judge, District Court of the United States for Porto Rico
1904 Photograph
Library of Congress

José Ramon Fernandez Savage
United States Attorney
From 1922 Passport Application
National Archives and Records Administration

October Term, 1907.

In the District Court of the United States for Porto Rico

Present: the Honorable Bernard S. Rodey, Judge.

March 31, 1908

Among the proceedings had were the following to wit:

The United States
vs.
Alexander Dickson.

Be it remembered that heretofore, to wit, on the 18th day of March, 1908, came the Grand Jury into Court and presented an indictment endorsed "A True Bill" against the Defendant Alexander Dickson, which said indictment is as follows: to wit:

United States of America } S.S.
District of Porto Rico

In the District Court of the United States, in and for the District aforesaid, at the October Term thereof, A. D. 1907.

The Grand Jurors of the United States, impaneled, sworn, and charged at the Term aforesaid, of the court aforesaid on their oath present that Alexander Dickson on the 20th day of February, in the year 1908 in the bay of San Juan, Porto Rico within the admiralty and maritime jurisdiction of the United States of America and out of the jurisdiction of any particular state thereof and within the jurisdiction of this court, in and on board of a certain vessel of the United States of America, to wit the Steamship called the "Aborada", which said vessel was then and there owned by the said United States of America, with force and arms unlawfully, feloniously and willfully did make an assault in and upon one Walter Weichert; and that the said Alexander Dickson, then and there, to wit, in the bay of San Juan, Porto Rico, within the admiralty and maritime jurisdiction of the United States of America and without the jurisdiction of any particular state thereof, and within the jurisdiction of this Court, in and on board of the said vessel, with a certain axe him the said Walter Weichert, in and upon the right thigh of him, the said Walter Weichert, and in and upon the left side of the jaw and nose of him the said Walter Weichert, unlawfully, feloniously and willfully did strike and penetrated and wound thereby, then and there, to wit in the bay of San Juan, Porto Rico, within the admiralty and maritime jurisdiction of any particular state thereof.

At a Stated Term of the District Court of the United States for Porto Rico Div. begun and holden at the Court on Monday, the October A.D. 1908, being the [illegible] day of said month, in the year of our Lord one thousand nine hundred and eight, and of the Independence of the United States of America the one hundred and thirty-third:

Present, the Honorable Bernard S. Rodey, Judge.

Among the proceedings had were the following, to wit:

October 26, 1908.

The United States
vs.
George Worley.

Be it remembered that heretofore, to wit: on the 4th day of March, A.D. 1908, came the Grand Jury into Court and presented an Indictment endorsed a "True bill" against the defendant George Worley, which said indictment is as follows, to wit:

United States of America }
District of Porto Rico }

In the District Court of the United States in and for the District aforesaid, at the October Term thereof, A.D. 1907.

The Grand Jurors of the United States [illegible] sworn and charged at the Term aforesaid, of the court aforesaid, on their oath present that George Worley [illegible] about the 10th day of February, in the year [illegible] on the high seas, within the admiralty and maritime jurisdiction of the United States of America and not of the jurisdiction of any particular State, County, and within the jurisdiction of this Court, in and on board of a certain vessel of the United States of America, to wit, the steamship called the "Abarenda" which said vessel was then and there owned by the said United States of America, with force and arms, in and upon J.H. Barnes did make an assault, and him the said J.H. Barnes then and there did unlawfully and willfully beat and illtreat, without justifiable cause; he the said George Worley being then and there the master of said vessel, and the said J.H. Barnes then and then a member of and one of the crew of the said said vessel, contrary to the form of the statute in such case made and provided, and against the peace and dignity of the United States.

[signed] United States Attorney

George W. Worley, Master, Collier *Abarenda*
Naval History and Heritage Command

who have been suddenly cut short of a bright future that was theirs by right. and no possible means of maintanance unless the pension to us is granted in recognition of the faithful service as a soldier, wounded in battle, also his splendid record as an officer in the governments Naval Auxil. U.S.S. Alexander, Hannabal, Brutus, and Alarenda, the recommendations from each are in my possession.

Mr. Commissioner, I beg of you to act generously in this worthy and needy cause. A favorable answer from you means everything to this heartbroken widow and babies of Walter Weichert.

A heart-felt appreciation of you will ever be from.

Yours, in sorrow.

Viola R. Weichert.
227 North St.
J. C Heights

"A heart-felt appreciation of you will ever be from, Yours, in sorrow, Viola R. Weichert"

Closing page of letter from Viola R. Weichert to V. Warner, Commissioner of Pensions
Pension file no. 925721, Walter R. Weichert, RG 15
National Archives and Records Administration

61st CONGRESS, } HOUSE OF REPRESENTATIVES. { REPORT
3d Session.   No. 1800.

VIOLA WEICHERT.

DECEMBER 20, 1910.—Ordered to be printed.

Mr. ADAIR, from the Committee on Claims, submitted the following

ADVERSE REPORT.

[To accompany H. R. 25613.]

The Committee on Claims, to whom was referred the bill (H. R. 25613) for the relief of Viola Weichert, widow of Walter R. Weichert, late chief officer of the U. S. naval auxiliary *Abarenda*, having considered the same, report thereon with a recommendation that it do not pass.

Upon a careful reading of the reports and testimony in this case, which are too voluminous to print, the committee is compelled to make an adverse report.

The report from the Navy Department is hereto attached and made a part of this report.

DEPARTMENT OF THE NAVY,
OFFICE OF THE SECRETARY,
Washington, May 13, 1910.

MY DEAR CONGRESSMAN: Referring to the bill (H. R. 25613) for the relief of Viola Weichert by paying her $5,000 in full compensation for the death of her husband, Walter Robert Weichert, late chief officer of the U. S. naval auxiliary *Abarenda*, who was killed on board that vessel February 20, 1908, by the ship's carpenter, Alexander Dickson, I have the honor to inclose herewith extracts from the record of proceedings of a board of inquest in the case, convened on board the *Abarenda* in the harbor of San Juan, P. R., on the day of Chief Officer Weichert's death, showing that Weichert was killed by Carpenter Dickson during or immediately after a controversy between the two men over an order issued by Weichert.

Dickson was tried at San Juan under indictment of March 18, 1908, on a charge of manslaughter and acquitted on the 31st of March.

The question as to whether Mr. Weichert's widow should under these circumstances be afforded relief by the Government is one that the department prefers to leave, without recommendation, to the committee's judgment.

Faithfully, yours,

BEEKMAN WINTHROP,
Acting Secretary.

Hon. GEORGE W. PRINCE, M. C.,
Chairman Committee on Claims, House of Representatives.

O

Reissue

3—732

Cert. No. 925-721

Mrs ACT OF JULY 16, 1918

Viola R

widow of

Walter R Weichert

Rank Pvt
Company D
Regiment 9 U S Inf

Rate per Month $ 12
Commencing Nov. 2, 1918 &
$20 per mo from Sept. 1, 1922
and $ 2 & 4 per month additional
Ending for 3 minor's as per brief.

Agency or Group No. } Gr 1

Issued May 4, 1923.

Pension approved for Mrs. Viola R. Weichert
Pension file no. 925721, Walter R. Weichert,
RG 15, National Archives and Records Administration

Robert L. Patterson
Undated Photograph
Courtesy, Vincent J. Patterson,
Great Nephew of Robert L. Patterson

HOMER BIRD

The Daily Picayune, New Orleans, Louisiana
November 18, 1902, Page 3

Murder in Klondike - 1898

The Saint Paul Globe, Saint Paul, Minnesota,
July 30, 1899, p. 8

Widow's Pension

Soon after the loss of her husband, Mrs. Viola Weichert, aged 29, sought much needed relief to support herself and her three young children. She believed that because her husband's death occurred in the line of duty on a federal ship and because of his prior service in the United States Army, during the Spanish-American War, and later on several ships of the U.S. Navy, that she would be eligible for a widow's pension from the United States government. The agency that managed the process was the Bureau of Pensions which was then part of the Department of the Interior.[180]

Viola Weichert of 227 North Street, Jersey City, New Jersey filed her first application, *Declaration of a Widow for Original Pension*, for a pension on March 7, 1908; less than a month after her husband's murder. She answered the numerous questions concerning her husband's service and about her marriage and children. The document signing was witnessed by two persons known to her: Hermann Peperkorn, who lived in the same building as Mrs. Weichert and Paul Becker who lived several blocks from her residence. The form was attested to by a Notary Public of the State of New Jersey. The form was date stamped, as received, at the U.S. Pension Office on March 14, 1908. It also contained a second stamp, same date, "Congressional U.S. Bureau of Pensions".[181]

---

[180] Department of the Interior, Bureau of Pensions form 3-333, in use March 21, 1908, Pension file no. 925721, Walter R. Weichert, Record Group 15, National Archives Building, Washington, DC

[181] Pension file no. 925721, Walter R. Weichert, Record Group 15, National Archives Building, Washington, DC

Members of the United States Congress attempted twice to provide a pension to the widow of Walter Weichert through the submission of Private Bills.

Private Bill (H. R. 18671) Granting a Pension to Viola Weichert

March 3, 1908 – Mr. Leake[182] of New Jersey introduced House of Representatives Bill (H. R.) 18671 Granting a Pension to Viola Weichert - to the Committee on Pensions.[183]

No further appearance of the Bill in later editions of the *Congressional Record* or *Statues at Large* indicates that it failed to pass.

The Navy Department was contacted by the Bureau of Pensions, regarding Walter Weichert's murder and service record. That request was forwarded to the Supervisor of Naval Auxiliaries on March 24, 1908.[184] That request was then forwarded to George Worley, Master of the *Abarenda*; and to one of Weichert's former commanding officers, George McDonald, Master of the *Brutus*. E.B. Barry, Supervisor of Naval Auxiliaries, summarized the responses to the Bureau of Navigation:

"Walter R. Weichert, born May 20, 1874[185], in New York, N.Y. made application for the position of First or Second Officer in the Naval Auxiliary Service on September 28, 1906. He passed satisfactory physical examination May 11, 1907, and was appointed Second Officer of the BRUTUS, May 16, 1907 to take

---

[182] Leake, Eugene, Walter, *Biographical Directory of the United States Congress*, website, http://bioguide.congress.gov/scripts/biodisplay.pl?index=L000175

[183] *Congressional Record*, Vol. 42, 60st Congress, 1st Session, March 3, 1908, p. 2852

[184] 1st Endorsement, Request from Rear Admiral J.E. Pillsbury, Chief, Bureau of Navigation to Supervisor of Naval Auxiliaries, March 24, 1908, Pension file no. 925721, Walter R. Weichert, Record Group 15, National Archives Building, Washington, DC

[185] The year of birth differs from the 1873 reference in his Army records.

effect May 20, 1907. He was promoted to the grade of First Officer and transferred to the U.S.S. ABARENDA, Dec. 1, 1907. His record has always been very good and excellent. Further information is not obtainable from the files of this office." [186] There was no reference; however, to Walter Weichert's service on board the *Alexander* or *Hannibal* which his widow cited in her pension application.

> March 13, 1908 – Congressman Eugene W. Leake of New Jersey wrote to the Commissioner of Pensions:[187]
> My dear Sir:-
> In accordance with your recent letter I have forwarded to Mrs. Weichert the declaration, which I am sending you herewith.
> May I respectfully ask that early consideration be given this matter, as the bill for a pension to Mrs. Weichert in the House of Representatives is awaiting the determination of your Department in this matter.
> Moreover the case is an exceedingly sad one. The husband of this woman was murdered while on the Naval Auxiliary Abarenda and the widow is left with three children, the oldest of which is less than six years of age.
> Very Respectfully,
> Eugene W. Leake"

March 23, 1908 - The Commissioner of Pensions informed Congressman C.V. Fornes of New York[188] that he awaited a reply

---

[186] 6th Endorsement. March 30, 1908. Subject: Bureau of Pensions. Response from Captain E.B. Barry, Supervisor of Naval Auxiliaries to Rear Admiral J.E. Pillsbury, Chief, Bureau of Navigation. Pension file no. 925721, Walter R. Weichert, Record Group 15, National Archives Building, Washington, DC
[187] Pension file no. 925721, Walter R. Weichert, Record Group 15, National Archives Building, Washington, DC
[188] Fornes, Charles Vincent, Biographical Directory of the United States Congress, website:
http://bioguide.congress.gov/scripts/biodisplay.pl?index=F000277

from the Navy's Bureau of Navigation concerning Walter R. Weichert.[189]

March 27, 1908 – The Bureau of Pensions wrote to Mrs. Weichert as they were unable to locate Walter Weichert listed "on the rolls of any company of the 9th regiment, New York Infantry, during the Spanish War…" She was requested to provide his certificate of discharge to the Bureau.[190]

March 31, 1908 – Mrs. Weichert wrote to the Commissioner of Pensions:[191]

At the top of the note was added: "Will you kindly return the enclosed newspaper clipping as I would like to keep it."

"Jersey City Heights, Mar 31/08
Commissioner V. Warner,
Dear Sir,

In reply to yours of Mar. 27th, must say that I am surprised you have not found a record of my husband's service and wound in the battle of San Diago [sic] where he enlisted in Comp D. Ninth Reg. under Capt. Powell (if I remember his name correctly). The honorable discharge paper, a dilapidated looking sheep skin also a letter sent to my husband from the War Dept. correcting the position of his wound, to the right arm, instead of left, over the signature of the Capt. of that Reg. Company, as my husband had requested that correction, these two papers I placed in the hands of the Hon. Eugene Leake, ~~Perhaps the~~ attached to my Declaration for Pension. I am writing to him also asking that he kindly hand these two papers over for your information.

On the certificate of honorable discharge, though partly eaten by a rat, the Notary Public who filled out the declaration, and I were able to read distinctly, the enlistment of Walter

---

[189] Pension file no. 925721, Walter R. Weichert, Record Group 15, National Archives Building, Washington, DC
[190] Pension file no. 925721, Walter R. Weichert, Record Group 15, National Archives Building, Washington, DC
[191] Pension file no. 925721, Walter R. Weichert, Record Group 15, National Archives Building, Washington, DC

Weichert June 26th 1898, at Cuba. I do not remember which (San Juan? Or San Diago) Comp. D. Ninth Reg. N.Y. Inft. Wounded in Battle of San Diago [sic] July 1, 1898 left arm on certificate of Discharge, but corrected later by War Dept. the other wounds in abdomen healed before he was discharged so record of it was taken. The paper gives his full description. Height 5 ft. 8 in. black hair, brown eyes, dark complexion[,] character, sober faithful.

After being wounded he was brought back to the U.S. where he received his honorable discharge. Doesn't that certificate of discharge answer fully the questions you ask. Mr. Weichert left his position as 2nd mate of a ship which was at Cuba during the war when he enlisted in the Reg. mentioned as Walter Weichert. I do hope you will have no difficulty in finding these facts which would entitle me and my three little ones to a relief from the government.

Can you realize Mr. Commissioner, what an utter helpless position, the brutal taking of my husband's life, while on duty as Chief Officer aboard the U.S.S. Abarenda has placed me in with three helpless babies the oldest, not 4 years till June, and the nursing enfant but 6 months who have been suddenly cut short of a bright future that was theirs by right and no possible means of maintenance unless the pension to me is granted in recognition of the faithful service as a soldier, wounded in battle, also his splendid record as an officer in the government's Naval Auxiliaries U.S.S. Alexander, Hannibal, Brutus and Abarenda, the recommendations from each are in my possession.

Mr. Commissioner, I beg of you to act generously in this worthy and needy cause. A favorable answer from you means everything to this heartbroken widow and babies of Walter Weichert.

A heart-felt appreciation of you will ever be from,
Yours, in sorrow,
Viola R. Weichert

227 North St.
J.C. Heights, N.J."

April 13, 1908 – Mrs. Weichert wrote to the Commissioner of Pensions:[192]

"227 North Street
Jersey City
Commissioner V. Warner,
Dear Sir,

I am pleased to learn through your letter of April 9th, that you have located the service of my husband Walter Weichert in ~~the~~ Co. D 9th regiment, U.S. Infantry. The mistake I made that he enlisted in the Volunteer Infantry of N.Y. was on account of drawing up the Declaration before the certificate of discharge was delivered to me from the U.S.S. Abarenda. I was under the impression that he had enlisted as a Volunteer. In reference to the mention in the newspaper clipping that he had rendered service during the Venesuelan [sic] disturbance during the administration of Pres. Cleveland must say that the information must have been given in an interview with some of my husband's friends who seem to know more about it than I do. I remember having heard him say that he had served before the Span Am. War during a Brazilian affair or perhaps it was the Venesuelan [sic] disturbance. I do not recall which. I regret to say that I find no paper referring to it. Perhaps it was lost among other papers in a ship wreck 1903. He remarked afterwards he was glad he didn't lose the old army discharge which had been in the possession of his sister.

We had frequently spoken over his experience in the San Diago [sic] battle especially at times when he suffered Rheumatic pains in his arm, a Boston physician said due to the nerves and sinews of the forearm being affected by the bullet that passed through the arm. The arm was quite disabled when ever he had an attack.

---

[192] Pension file no. 925721, Walter R. Weichert, Record Group 15, National Archives Building, Washington, DC

Trusting that you will soon be able to make a favorable decision for the relief of myself and the three little ones. I beg to remain,

    Respectfully yours,
    Viola Weichert"

W.R. Shoemaker, Commander, U.S. Navy reported that Walter Weichert's Venezuelan role could not be substantiated by the Navy Department. "While it appears that several vessels touched a Venezuelan port in the course of the of cruises during the last administration of President Cleveland, it is not shown that any one was "stationed" in those waters during that time. When the trouble with Venezuela occurred in August 1892, the "Kearsarge" and "Concord" were sent there, and the "Chicago" was off Venezuela in September and October 1892 for the protection of American interests, but examination of the muster rolls of the vessels named for the third and fourth quarters of 1892 fails to discover the name Walter R. Weichert."[193]

Captain E.B. Barry, Supervisor of Naval Auxiliaries wrote to the Commissioner of Pensions that, "Under the date of July 9, 1903, W. R. Weichert wrote

"I also wish to state that I have served in the U.S. Army during the war with Spain, for the term of four and one half months, and holding an honorable discharge, was wounded in three places during the battle of San Juan, and if necessary will enclose the discharge for inspection." and in his application of the same date for First or Second Officer under "Voyages performed" are mentioned (Position) 2nd Officer; (vessel) U.S.N.C. Hannibal;

---

[193] Correspondence, 4th Endorsement, from W.R. Shoemaker, Commander, U.S. Navy to the Commissioner of Pensions, October 10, 1908, Pension file no. 925721, Record Group 15; National Archives Bldg., Washington, DC

(date) 1901; (voyage) 6 mos." And (Position) 2nd Officer; (vessel) U.S.N.C. Alexander; (date) 1902; (voyage) 6 mos."""[194]

April 21, 1908 – Martha Weichert-Klee, age 36 (sister of Walter Weichert) and her husband[195] Henry Klee, age 60, of 58 9th Avenue, New York City swore before a Notary Public as to how they were related to the deceased and that he had not been married prior to his marriage to Viola R. Patterson.[196]

April 24, 1908 – Herman Peperkorn and Paul Becker of Jersey City, New Jersey attested on a sworn affidavit that they both knew the widow Weichert and commented as others had about her marriage to Walter Weichert. Also on that day, Mrs. Mary A. Love of Boston Massachusetts attested to the same information.[197]

May 1, 1908 – The Commissioner of Pensions requested that Mrs. Weichert provide an additional affidavit from an additional witness who could attest that she had never been married prior to her marriage to Walter R. Weichert.[198]

May 6, 1908 – Mrs. Weichert wrote to the Bureau of Pensions:[199]
> "Commissioner V. Warner
> Dear Sir,
> Enclosed please find testimony of credible witnesses, as requested in par. 9, also certificate of baptism for my youngest child. I have written to Dr. McCarthy of East

---

[194] Correspondence, 3rd Endorsement from E.B.B. Barry, Supervisor of Naval Auxiliaries to the Commissioner of Pensions, August 29, 1908, Pension file no. 925721, Record Group 15; National Archives Bldg., Washington, DC
[195] Martha Klee (nee Weichert) and Henry Klee were married on June 7, 1892 in New York City, NY, Certificate Number: 7196, New York City Department of Records
[196] Pension file no. 925721, Walter R. Weichert, Record Group 15, National Archives Building, Washington, DC
[197] Pension file no. 925721, Walter R. Weichert, Record Group 15, National Archives Building, Washington, DC
[198] Pension file no. 925721, Walter R. Weichert, Record Group 15, National Archives Building, Washington, DC
[199] Pension file no. 925721, Walter R. Weichert, Record Group 15, National Archives Building, Washington, DC

Boston, who was the attending physician at the births of my first and second child, asking him to obtain the public record of their births in that city and kindly forward to you, also the testimony of one more witness from New Orleans, that I was never married before, will be forwarded in a few days. Trusting Mr. Commissioner that you will soon be able to give a favorable report, that a speedy relief may come to these three little ones and myself. I thank you most sincerely for prompt attention you have so far given my claim.
    Very Truly Yours,
    Viola R. Weichert"

May 8, 1908 –
Sworn before a Notary Public: "Mr. Jeff. D. Patterson, a resident of this city of New Orleans being by me duly sworn says that he is the paternal uncle of Viola Ruth Patterson now the widow of Walter Robert Weichert; that he has known the said Viola Ruth Weichert all her life and knows that she was never married prior to her marriage with said Walter Robert Weichert, which was celebrated in this city on or about April 21, 1903.
Jeff. D. Patterson
age, 47 years
1652 N. Broad Street
New Orleans, La
Sworn and subscribed before me on this 8th day of May 1908.
Bernard Titche
Notary"[200]

Sworn before a Notary Public:
"State of Louisiana, Parish of Orleans, City of New Orleans

---

[200] Pension file no. 925721, Walter R. Weichert, Record Group 15, National Archives Building, Washington, DC

Bernard Titche being duly sworn says that he was well acquainted with the late Robert L. Patterson. That Viola Ruth Patterson widow of Walter Robert Weichert is his daughter; that he was the legal advisor of said Viola Ruth Patterson for a few years prior to her marriage ; that he has never heard of any other marriage having been contracted than that with said Walter Robert Weichert in this city on or about April 21, 1903. That he was present at said marriage and believes that had said Miss Viola Patterson ever been married prior thereto, he must have known of it.
Bernard Titche
age 49 years
Res. 1929 Napoleon Ave., New Orleans, La
Sworn and subscribed before me on this 8th day of May, 1908
Bertrand Cahn
Notary Public"[201]

Sworn before a Notary Public:
Doctor T.F. McCarthy of East Boston, Massachusetts provided certificates of birth for two of the Weichert children who were born in Boston and attested to supportive information concerning their birth.[202]

May 11, 1908 – The Commissioner of Pensions wrote to Congressman James A. Hamill of New Jersey[203] concerning the need for Mrs. Weichert to provide the testimony of a witness of the fact that she had not been married before her marriage to Walter R. Weichert. She would also need to provide testimony as well concerning the birth of two children.[204]

---

[201] Pension file no. 925721, Walter R. Weichert, Record Group 15, National Archives Building, Washington, DC
[202] Pension file no. 925721, Walter R. Weichert, Record Group 15, National Archives Building, Washington, DC
[203] Hamill, James Alphonsus, *Biographical Directory of the United States Congress*, website:
http://bioguide.congress.gov/scripts/biodisplay.pl?index=H000099
[204] Pension file no. 925721, Walter R. Weichert, Record Group 15, National Archives Building, Washington, DC

May 15, 1908 – Mrs. Weichert sent a postal card to Commissioner
V. Warner, Bureau of Pensions:[205]
"227 North St.
Jersey City Heights
Commissioner Warner,
   Will you kindly send me a card if the last testimony requested in May 1st, has been received namely, 2 public records of birth for two of my children from Boston, Mass, also of one witness as to my non prior marriage which was mailed to you from New Orleans, La! Congressman Jos. Hammil [sic] said you had not received it up to Monday last.
Respectfully,
Viola R. Weichert

May 20, 1908 – The Commissioner of Pensions informed Mrs. Weichert that he waited for a reply from the Navy Department relative to her husband's service.[206]

November 18, 1908 - Mrs. Viola Weichert wrote to Commissioner
Warner, Commissioner of Pensions.[207]
"227 North St.
Jersey City Heights
Nov. 18/08

---

[205] Wid Orig. 26.707 Walter R. Weichert. U.S. Navy, Pension file no. 925721, Walter R. Weichert, Record Group 15, National Archives Building, Washington, DC

[206] Pension file no. 925721, Walter R. Weichert, Record Group 15, National Archives Building, Washington, DC

[207] Notations handwritten on letter: A.& N. Div., W.O. 26707, Viola R. Weichert, Walter R. Weichert; Ink stamps on letter from U.S. Government offices: (Round) U.S. Pension Office NOV 19 1908, (Oval) Finance Division, Bureau of Pensions *NOV 20 1908*., (Rectangular) Army and Navy Division Files NOV 21 1908 Received, Pension file no. 925721, Walter R. Weichert, Record Group 15, National Archives Building, Washington, DC

Commissioner Warner,
Honorable Sir,

I have received your letter of the 17th informing me that my claim for pension under the general law is rejected on the ground that my husband was a civilian employee and not an enlisted man in the Navy.

Certainly my husband was not an enlisted man in the Navy. Having met his death as an employee of the government on a U.S. Navy Auxiliary, I was under the impression that the claim was marked U.S. Navy, and that some recompense may be given also on account of that fact. The grounds upon which I have based my claim for pension and for which I have furnished the positive proofs, is the fact that he was an enlisted man in the Regular U.S. Infantry, Comp. D. under Capt. Powell and was wounded in the battle of Saniago [sic] in Span-Am. War and on account of his wounds was honorably discharged.

You have that certificate in your possession, commissioner, also the letter from the U.S. Adjutant[208] General, to my husband relative to the wound received in battle. Do not these facts entitle me to a right to relief from the government for my self [sic] and these three little helpless babies. Is there not a new law which is to provide a pension for every soldier of the Span-Am. War? Has not this widow and orphans of a soldier wounded in battle, more right to a pension when all necessary proofs have been submitted. The different Congressmen who have offered their assistance in my behalf, especially the Hon. Leake and Hamlin of N. Jersey feel that I have sufficient grounds for a pension. Honorable sir, will you not relieve my great distress by an early reply to this.

I beg of you to reconsider my case, and see in it the justice due me and my little ones. Trusting to receive an encouraging reply. I am
    Yours, in distress,
    (Mrs.) Viola R. Weichert"

---

[208] Was written as "Ajacent" in letter.

November 24, 1908 - The Pension Bureau returned several items to Mrs. Weichert: a newspaper clipping; discharge certificate and personal papers that she filed with her claim for pension.[209]

November 28, 1908 - The Commissioner of Pensions informed Congressman Hamill that Mrs. Weichert's claim for pension was rejected as her husband was a civilian employee of the Navy and not an officer nor an enlisted man. That rejection was conveyed to Mrs. Weichert by the Commissioner on December 2, 1908.[210]

March 12, 1909 - Congressman James A. Hamill wrote to J. L. Davenport, Commissioner of Pensions:[211]
My dear Mr. Davenport,
    I enclose to you herewith application for pension of Viola Ruth Weichert as widow of Walter Robert Weichert, whose post office address is No. 227 North Street, Jersey City. Will you kindly acknowledge receipt of it and let me know what evidence you will require to establish the claim and I will endeavor to procure it. Thanking you for your prompt attention to this matter."

March 19, 1909 – The Bureau of Pensions decided that the Mrs. Weichert's claim for pension should be based upon her husband's Army service.[212]

---

[209] Pension file no. 925721, Walter R. Weichert, Record Group 15, National Archives Building, Washington, DC
[210] Pension file no. 925721, Walter R. Weichert, Record Group 15, National Archives Building, Washington, DC
[211] Pension file no. 925721, Walter R. Weichert, Record Group 15, National Archives Building, Washington, DC
[212] Bureau of Pensions records jacket, Claim W.O. 26,707, stamped by the Records Division on March 22, 1909. Pension file no. 925721, Walter R. Weichert, Record Group 15, National Archives Building, Washington, DC

April 24, 1909 - The Commissioner of Pension informed Mrs. Weichert that her claim was rejected because the murder of her husband "had no connection with his military service."[213]

Private Bill (H. R. 25613) for the Relief of Viola Weichert

May 7, 1910 - Mr. Kinkead[214] of New Jersey introduced House of Representatives Bill (H. R.) 25613 for the relief of Viola Weichert [215]

May 13, 1910 - The Navy Department responded to a Congressional inquiry related to the Bill:

"Department of the Navy
Office of the Secretary
Washington, May 13, 1910

My Dear Congressman: Referring to the bill (H. R. 25613) for the relief of Viola Weichert by paying her $5,000 in full compensation for the death of her husband, Walter Robert Weichert, late chief officer of the U.S. naval auxiliary *Abarenda*, who was killed on board that vessel February 20, 1908, by the ship's carpenter, Alexander Dickson, I have the honor to inclose [sic] herewith extracts from the record of proceedings of a board of inquest in the case, convened on board the *Abarenda* in the harbor of San Juan, P.R., on the day of Chief Officer Weichert's death, showing that Weichert was killed by Carpenter Dickson during or immediately after a controversy between the two men over an order issued by Weichert. Dickson was tried at San Juan under indictment of March 18, 1908, on a charge of manslaughter

---

[213] Pension file no. 925721, Walter R. Weichert, Record Group 15, National Archives Building, Washington, DC
[214] Kinkead, Eugene Francis, *Biographical Directory of the United States Congress*, website: http://bioguide.congress.gov/scripts/biodisplay.pl?index=K000222
[215] *Congressional Record*, Vol. 45, 61st Congress, 2nd Session, May 7, 1910, p. 5940

and acquitted on the 31st of March. The question as to whether Mr. Weichert's widow should under these circumstances be afforded relief by the Government is one that the department prefers to leave, without recommendation, to the committee's judgment.

Hon. George W. Prince, M.C.,
Chairman Committee on Claims, House of Representatives [216]

Faithfully, yours,
Beekman Winthrop,
Acting Secretary"[217]

June 6, 1910 – Congressman Kinkead to Congressman Adair:

"My Dear Congressman:-
Referring now to the Weichert case I beg to inform you that I know the widow, Mrs. Viola Weichert, and I know that she is in very needy circumstances. The death of her husband in the line of duty in the quartermaster's service[218] left her without means of support for herself and her young family. As suggested I spoke to Mr. Prince, and I am having the Navy Department send to your committee all the information which they have on hand showing the causes leading up to the trouble which ended in the death of

---

[216] Department of the Navy response to Congressional inquiry; part of House of Representatives Report No. 1800, Adverse Report, H. R. 25613, 61st Congress, 3rd Session, December 20, 1910

[217] Correspondence from Beekman Winthrop, Acting Secretary, Department of the Navy, to Prince, George Washington, Chairman, Committee on Claims, House of Representatives, May 13, 1910, part of House of Representatives Report No. 1800, Adverse Report, H. R. 25613, 61st Congress, 3rd Session, December 20, 1910

[218] The reference to the Quartermaster's Service was in error.

Weichert. Thanking you for the interest you have manifested in this matter."[219]

June 7, 1910 - Mrs. Weichert's local newspaper reported that, "Congressman Eugene F. Kinkead was before the House Committee on Claims yesterday urging the passage of a bill which he has introduced in behalf of Mrs. Viola Weichert, whose husband Walter Robert Weichert, late chief officer of the United States Auxiliary "Abarenda," was killed in the service, and whose tragic death occurred two years ago. The claim was first presented by Congressman Leake. The Committee on Claims has not passed many bills of this character during the present session, but Kinkead is hopeful of getting through a favorable report on the bill."[220]

June 11, 1910 - Beekman Winthrop, Acting Navy Secretary informed Congressman Prince that a request had been made of the Justice Department for a transcript of the Dickson trial.[221]

July 11, 1910 - Beekman Winthrop, Acting Navy Secretary informed Congressman Prince that the Navy Department received the requested court transcript and included it with their correspondence.[222]

---

[219] Correspondence, Congressman Kinkead to Congressman Adair, June 6, 1910, Record Group 233; National Archives Bldg., Washington, DC
[220] Kinkead Pleads for Weichert's Widow, *The Jersey Journal*, Jersey City, NJ, June 7, 1910, p. 3
[221] Correspondence from Beekman Winthrop, Acting Secretary, Department of the Navy, to Prince, George Washington, Chairman, Committee on Claims, House of Representatives, Record Group 233; National Archives Bldg., Washington, DC
[222] Correspondence from Beekman Winthrop, Acting Secretary, Department of the Navy, to Prince, George Washington, Chairman, Committee on Claims, House of Representatives, Record Group 233; National Archives Bldg., Washington, DC

December 20, 1910 – "Mr. Adair (Representative from Indiana[223]) from the Committee on Claims, to which was referred the bill of the House (H. R. 25613) for the relief of Viola Weichert, reported the same adversely, accompanied by a report (No. 1800), which said bill and report were laid on the table."[224]

February 2, 1911 – Mrs. Weichert request that Commissioner Warner return the copy of her husband's Honorable Discharge certificate that she provided two years earlier. Her new address, 174 Lincoln St. Jersey City Heights, N.J.[225]

"ADVERSE REPORT
(To accompany H. R. 25613)

The Committee on Claims to whom was referred the bill (H. R. 25613) for the relief of Viola Weichert, widow of Walter R. Weichert, late chief officer of the U.S. naval auxiliary *Abarenda*, having considered the same report thereon with a recommendation that it do not pass. Upon a careful reading of the reports and testimony in this case, which are too voluminous to print, the committee is compelled to make an adverse report. The report from the Navy Department is hereto attached and made a part of this report."[226]

---

[223] Adair, John Alfred McDowell, *Biographical Directory of the United States Congress*, website, http://bioguide.congress.gov/scripts/biodisplay.pl?index=A000027

[224] *Congressional Record*, Vol. 46, 61st Congress, 3rd Session, December 20, 1910, p. 542

[225] Pension file no. 925721, Walter R. Weichert, Record Group 15, National Archives Building, Washington, DC

[226] House of Representatives Report No. 1800, Adverse Report, H. R. 25613, 61st Congress, 3rd Session, December 20, 1910

November 8, 1917 – Mrs. Weichert wrote to the Commissioner of Pensions, Washington, D.C.[227]

"Hon. Sir,

I have been informed that a law was passed by Congress and went into effect Oct. 6th last granting a pension to widows of soldiers who had active service during the Spanish - Am - war. Will you kindly advise me if this is so, and if I am eligible for same? My husband was wounded at Sandiago [sic] and some years later was killed on one of the Naval Auxiliary ships in the employ of the government. He was 1st Officer of the U.S.S. Abarenda. I have three little children.

    Kindly oblige
    (Mrs.) Viola Weichert
    338 East 65 St.
    New York City"

November 30, 1917 - Commissioner Saltzgaber, Bureau of Pensions wrote to Mrs. Weichert:[228]

"…I have to advise you that the act of October 6, 1917, does not grant title to original pension, but provides for an increase of pension only to a widow of an officer or enlisted man of the Army, Navy or Marine Corps of the United States who served in the Civil War, the War with Spain or the Philippine Insurrection."

October 30, 1918 - Mrs. Weichert's application for pension was submitted through Congressman Carew's office.[229]

---

[227] Pension file no. 925721, Walter R. Weichert, Record Group 15, National Archives Building, Washington, DC
[228] Pension file no. 925721, Walter R. Weichert, Record Group 15, National Archives Building, Washington, DC
[229] Pension file no. 925721, Walter R. Weichert, Record Group 15, National Archives Building, Washington, DC

April 30, 1919 - Congressman John F. Carew[230] of New York hand wrote a letter to the Commissioner of Pensions in which he conveys details of Walter Weichert's army service and Mrs. Weichert's insistence that her husband was wounded at the battle of Santiago. The Bureau's rejection of the pension claim was questioned. Mr. Carew also asked, "Is ninety days service outside of the United States required for a Spanish War Veterans widow to get a pension[?]"[231]

May 6, 1919 – Congressman John F. Carew hand wrote a letter to the Commissioner of Pensions in which he questioned the rejection of Mrs. Weichert's application for pension.[232]

May 12, 1919 – Acting Pension Commissioner E. C. Tieman wrote to Congressman Carew; that Mrs. Weichert's claim for pension was rejected on April 26, 1919 as her late husband "did not render ninety days actual military service in the War with Spain, the organization to which he belonged having been stationed in the United States during the entire period of his service except from the date of his enlistment, June 26, 1898, to August 4, 1898, a period of less than ninety days. A report from the records of the War Department showed that the soldier enlisted June 26, 1898, that he remained in Cuba until July 11, 1898, and that he was furloughed August 4, 1898, from Fort McPherson, Ga. This report has been reexamined, and there is nothing therein to indicate that soldier served over four months in Cuba, as stated by the claimant."[233]

---

[230] Carew, John Francis, *Biographical Directory of the United States Congress*, website, http://bioguide.congress.gov/scripts/biodisplay.pl?index=C000142
[231] Pension file no. 925721, Walter R. Weichert, Record Group 15, National Archives Building, Washington, DC
[232] Pension file no. 925721, Walter R. Weichert, Record Group 15, National Archives Building, Washington, DC
[233] Pension file no. 925721, Walter R. Weichert, Record Group 15, National Archives Building, Washington, DC

May 28, 1919 - Commissioner Saltzgaber, Bureau of Pensions wrote to Congressman Carew to inform him that Mrs. Weichert's application for pension was rejected because her husband "did not render ninety days actual military service in the War with Spain..."[234]

June 12, 1919 - Congressman Carew wrote to Commissioner Saltzgaber, Bureau of Pensions. He requested that the Commissioner "carefully read the law" and review his letter as the Congressman attempted to clarify details concerning Walter Weichert's military service. "...Weichert volunteered into the Regular Army for the Spanish War went to Cuba was wounded and returned home for wounds..." "If Weichert is not entitled to a pension because he volunteered into the Regular Army instead of a National Guard outfit the law is defective but I do not think it is. It says volunteers that means all volunteers no matter into what service they volunteered so long as they volunteered into service during that war[.] Volunteering to go whenever sent the law should be construed to pension them especially if as did Weichert they went to Cuba[.] They are not in the same category as men who were in the Regular Establishment before the war started and who simply fulfilled their previous contract of enlistment."[235]

June 21, 1919 - The Acting Commissioner of Pensions responded to Congressman Carew's letter and continued the defense of the Bureau's decision to reject Mrs. Weichert's application for pension.

---

[234] Pension file no. 925721, Walter R. Weichert, Record Group 15, National Archives Building, Washington, DC
[235] Pension file no. 925721, Walter R. Weichert, Record Group 15, National Archives Building, Washington, DC

March 22, 1922 - Mrs. Viola R. Weichert, age 39, 338 E. 65 St., Referred to Presbyterian Hospital Medical Clinic for treatment of stomach condition.[236]

September 17, 1922 - Congressman Carew hand wrote a letter to the Pension Office in which he stated his belief that Mrs. Weichert's claim is now valid and requests a clarification as to when the pension payments should be effective.[237]

September 27, 1922 - The Chief Clerk of the Bureau of Pensions informed Congressman Carew that Mrs. Weichert's claim for pension under the act of July 16, 1918 was rejected because her husband was only stationed outside of the U.S. from June 26, 1898 to August 14, 1898. She was to file a new application under the act of September 1, 1922.[238]

October 16, 1922 – Mrs. Weichert wrote to the Bureau of Pensions:[239]

"Hon. G.M. Saltzgaber
Commissioner of Pensions
Dear Sir,

By the request of Congressman John F. Carew of New York, who has received your communication, I am enclosing a copy of the Act of Sept[.] 1, 1922 relative to the Spanish War Veteran's Widow, Sec. 5. As to previous claim under Act of July 16, 1918. I have struggled along for 14 years bringing up my three children, since their father was killed on board U.S.S. Abarenda, and I

---

[236] Referral paper from Woman's Hospital, Social Service Department, Pension file no. 925721, Walter R. Weichert, Record Group 15, National Archives Building, Washington, DC
[237] Pension file no. 925721, Walter R. Weichert, Record Group 15, National Archives Building, Washington, DC
[238] Pension file no. 925721, Walter R. Weichert, Record Group 15, National Archives Building, Washington, DC
[239] Pension file no. 925721, Walter R. Weichert, Record Group 15, National Archives Building, Washington, DC

assure you that this pension, that I had hoped for all these years will be indeed quite a help.
Respectfully
(Mrs.) Viola R. Weichert
338 E. 65 St."

November 9, 1922 - Washington Gardner, Commissioner of Pensions advised Mrs. Weichert to provide "sworn statements of two witnesses, having personal knowledge of the facts, showing whether" she "ever remarried after the death of" her husband. In addition, statements from two witnesses, were also to be provided to the Bureau, showing whether her three children were still alive. "No affidavit can be considered satisfactory that fails to state the affiant's age, post office address and means of knowledge of the facts stated."[240]

November 18, 1922 -

Mr. Weichert informs the Commissioner of Pension of her move from 338 East 65th Street to 331 East 65th Street, New York City. On that date, Martha Klee, (nee Weichert), age 51 swore an affidavit attesting that she was Walter Weichert's sister and that, "I am a frequent visitor to the home of the widow Viola R. Weichert, age 39 yrs...." She also stated that the widow never remarried. She listed the names and dates of birth of Viola Weichert's children and that they were living and under the care of their mother.

Fifty two year old Thomas F. Nicholas of 309 E. 65th Street, employed by the New York City Department of Public Buildings, also swore an affidavit that stated that he was Mrs. Weichert's neighbor for the past 15 years. He also attested to the fact the Mrs.

---

[240] Pension file no. 925721, Walter R. Weichert, Record Group 15, National Archives Building, Washington, DC

Weichert never remarried and that her children were still living with her.[241]

December 10, 1922 - Mrs. Weichert wrote to the Commissioner of Pensions:[242]

"Hon. Washington Gardner
Commissioner of Pensions
Dear Sir,

In accordance with your request of Nov. 9th, I mailed then, the two sworn affidavits, as to, the fact that I had never remarried since the death of the soldier and that the three children are still living. The other required proofs have been on file in the Department for some time having been given by Congressman John F. Carew. Since the death of my husband in 1908 , I have waited and hoped each year that I would eventually receive some compensation that would assist me in giving the children a better life. My expenses have been very heavy recently, and I am going to ask this special favor[.] Dear Commissioner, that if possible, you will have my claim settled in time to give the children a much brighter Christmas. Thank you sincerely for kindness in the past.

Yours Respectfully,
Viola R. Weichert
331 East 65th St.
New York, N.Y."

December 15, 1922 - Washington Gardner, Commissioner of Pensions informed Mrs. Weichert that "relative to your claim Widow's Original Number 915470 as Widow of Walter R.

---

[241] Statement sworn before John F. Keeley, Notary Public, New York County, NY, Pension file no. 925721, Walter R. Weichert, Record Group 15, National Archives Building, Washington, DC

[242] Handwritten on stationery from the Board of Education, The City of New York, Bureau of Attendance, 154-156 68th Street, Pension file no. 925721, Walter R. Weichert, Record Group 15, National Archives Building, Washington, DC

Weichert, late of Company D, 9th United States Infantry, you are advised that your claim under the Act of September 1, 1922 has been allowed at the rate of $20 per month and $4 additional for the minor child, Viola R. commencing October 18, 1922, the date your application was filed in the bureau."[243]

December 30, 1922 - Robert C. Davis, Adjutant General, The War Department notified the Commissioner of Pensions that Walter Weichert "…was discharged Nov. 8, 1898, upon his own application, under the provisions of G.O.40, A.G.O 1898, on account of his being a married man."[244]

January 6, 1923 - Congressman John F. Carew[245] of New York hand wrote a letter to the Commissioner of Pensions in which he questioned the effective date of Mrs. Weichert's benefits.[246]

January 7, 1923 - Mrs. Weichert wrote to Congressman John F. Carew (Representative from New York):[247]
"Dear Mr. Carew,
In accordance with your suggestion on Saturday, I am enclosing the number of the Act of Sept. 1, 1922 – Public – No. 294, 67th Congress, H R 4 An act granting relief to Spanish War widows etc. Sec. 5. which reads that all widows' claims under the act of July 1918 (Spanish War Widows) which were rejected on account of the soldier not having spent 90 days on Foreign soil, in in the regular army, <u>will be entitled</u> to have their pension start from the date of the Original claim of 1918, at the rate of $12. Per mo[.] for widow and $2. For each minor child up to the

---

[243] Pension file no. 925721, Walter R. Weichert, Record Group 15, National Archives Building, Washington, DC
[244] Pension file no. 925721, Walter R. Weichert, Record Group 15, National Archives Building, Washington, DC
[245] Carew, John Francis, *Biographical Directory of the United States Congress*, website, http://bioguide.congress.gov
[246] Pension file no. 925721, Walter R. Weichert, Record Group 15, National Archives Building, Washington, DC
[247] Pension file no. 925721, Walter R. Weichert, Record Group 15, National Archives Building, Washington, DC

date of the claim under the act of Sept[.] 1, 1922 and from then on at the rate of $20. per mo. for w[id]ow and $4 for each minor child.

My original claim number Oct[.] 1918 was WO915470. The two enclosed cards will show that my new claim was given the number of original claim. Also all correspondence was marked with the original claim no. WO.915470.

The certificate of pension and voucher for first payment has been given a new number 925,721 and marked Original, and states that pension commences Oct[.] 18, 1922.

Mr. Carew, if you will kindly obtain a copy of the act, and see Commissioner Gardiner personally, I feel that you will be able to convince him that I am entitled to the back pay from my original claim of 1918.

With a sincere appreciation of all your favors of the past

I am Respectfully yours
   Viola R. Weichert
   331 East 65th St
   New York, N.Y."

January 17, 1923 – The Commissioner of Pensions advised Congressman Carew that Mr. Weichert "is pensioned under the act of September 1, 1922, under which act pension begins at the date of filing the application. Her pension thereunder was made to commence October 18, 1922. She filed a claim for pension under the act of July 16, 1918, on November 2, 1918, which was rejected in April 1919, on the ground that the soldier did not render 90 days actual military service in the war with Spain, the organization to which he belonged having been stationed in the United States during the entire period of his service except from the date of his enlistment June 26, 1898 to August 14, 1898. Her rejected claim is now under consideration with a view to determining whether reopening is warranted under a recent decision of the Honorable Secretary of the Interior. You and the claimant will be advised of the final result."[248]

January 23, 1923 – Mrs. Weichert wrote to Congressman John Marshall Robsion[249] of Kentucky:[250]

"331 East 65 St.
New York

Hon. John M. Robsion
House of Representatives

My dear Mr. Robsion,

Having read several times over the Congressional Record of Feb. 1, 1922, in which you so splendidly presented and worked for the passage of the Spanish War Pension Bill – H.R. 4. Public No. 294.67. I am taking this liberty as a southerner like yourself to write to ask if you will lend your assistance in my behalf. I feel confident that a word from you to the Secretary of the Interior Mr. Fall will have much weight in settling my claim for the back pay under the act of July 1918. My husband, Walter R. Weichert enlisted on the Battle fields of Cuba June 26, 1898 and was wounded in Battle of Sandiago [sic] (as shown on record of War Dept). He was placed in Comp D, 9th U.S. Infantry, although a volunteer, and served over 100 days before receiving his Honorable Discharge in Oct. 1898. Because he was placed in the regular army, and did not spend 90 days on foreign soil. My claim was rejected. As I read Sec 5, of the Act of Sept. 2, 1922, as to claims of Spanish War widows under act of July 1918, that have been rejected on the ground that 90 days service was not shown

---

[248] Correspondence from Commissioner [of Pensions] to Congressman John F. Carew, January 17, 1923, Pension file no. 925721, Walter R. Weichert, Record Group 15, National Archives Building, Washington, DC
[249] Robsion, John Marshall, website, http://bioguide.congress.gov/scripts/biodisplay.pl?index=R000358
[250] Pension file no. 925721, Walter R. Weichert, Record Group 15, National Archives Building, Washington, DC

exclusive of leave of absence or furlough, the pension shall begin from the date of when the original claim was filed. Does it not appear clearly to you Mr. Robsion, that I am entitled to my claim from 1918 under this Sec 5 of the act of 1922? Without the necessity of a special ruling or decision by the Hon. Secretary of the Interior? Whether my claim shall be opened or not? My husband as 1st Officer on U.S. Naval Collier Abarenda was killed, in the line of duty in Feb. 1908, for whose death I have never had a cent of compensation, though I was left with 3 children under 5 yrs of age. Each claim was rejected by the Bureau of Pensions. Now I will be deeply grateful to you if you can see Commissioner Gardiner or the Secretary of the Interior.
Very sincerely Viola R. Weichert"

January 25, 1923 - Congressman Robsion wrote to the Bureau of Pensions on behalf of Mrs. Weichert's claim for back pension, in which he stated, "I am sure you will give this claim your earnest consideration." Mr. Robsion was a member of the Committee on Pensions.[251]

January 27, 1923 - The Commissioner of Pensions advised Mrs. Weichert to provide her own sworn statement and the same from "two other persons having the requisite knowledge, showing the character, location and value of all property owned by her or in which she had any interest at the date of filing her claim, November 2, 1918, and the amount of her annual income not the result of her daily labor; also a statement by the proper official showing the assessed value of her real property, if any, for each year from 1918 to 1922."[252]

---

[251] Pension file no. 925721, Walter R. Weichert, Record Group 15, National Archives Building, Washington, DC
[252] Excerpt from correspondence from the Commissioner [of Pensions] to Congressman J.M. Robsion, February 8, 1923, Pension file no. 925721, Walter R. Weichert, Record Group 15, National Archives Building, Washington, DC

February 3, 1923 - A letter was written and provided to the Bureau of Pensions, Widow Division:[253]

    To Whom it May concern,

    This is to certify that Mrs[.] Viola Weichert has worked for me at intervals during the dates between Oct 1921 - and October 1922.

    Very truly
    Irving Coon

February 5, 1923: Two affidavits were sworn before a notary public and provided to the Bureau of Pensions, Widow Division:[254]

    "I[,] the said Terrence J. O'Donnell[,] have known Mrs. (Viola) Weichert of 331 East 65 St. for the past seven years and to my knowledge have known her to own no personal property Stock or Bonds. I[,] the said Terrence J. O'Donnell[,] Chairman[,] Relief Committee of Gen. Guy V. Henry Camp #38[,] United Spanish War Veterans extended monthly to the said Viola Weichert, relief from 1917 to 1920 inclusive for support for herself and children[.]

    Signed,
    Terrence J. O'Donnell
    316 East 55 St
    N.Y. City N.Y.
    Age 46 Years"

    "I, Thomas F. Nicholas have known Mrs. Viola R. Weichert for the past ten years and known her to own no property,

---

[253] Handwritten on the letterhead of Irving Coon, Appraiser and Auctioneer, 88 University Place, New York, Pension file no. 925721, Walter R. Weichert, Record Group 15, National Archives Building, Washington, DC

[254] Pension file no. 925721, Walter R. Weichert, Record Group 15, National Archives Building, Washington, DC

stocks or bonds. As Treasurer-Almoner[255] of the Relief Com[m]itte[e] of United Spanish War Veterans of New York County, I Recommended Mrs. Viola R. Weichert for Relief from the Spanish War Veterans fund, as she was unable to earn enough to support her self and three children on account of illness and a severe operation.

    Signed,
    Thomas F. Nicholas
    309 East 65th St.
    New York City, N.Y.
    Age 52 Years"

February 6, 1923 - An affidavit was sworn before a notary public and provided to the Bureau of Pensions, Widow Division:[256]

"I, Martha Klee (nee Weichert) age 51 years - living at 58 Ninth Ave N.Y.C. am the sister of the dead soldier Walter R. Weichert of comp. D. 9th U.S. Infantry. I took care of the three children of Viola R. Weichert during the time that she was in the hospital and convalescent hospital after a serious operation from Sept 18th to Nov 15th, of 1919. Mrs. Weichert has suffered cronic [sic] nervous trouble for years and was unable to earn sufficient to support her self and three children and often received financial assistance from me.

    Signed
    Martha Klee
    New-York, Feb 6th 1923"

---

[255] Definitions: *Almoner* - "One who distributes alms for another" p. 21; *Alms* - "1. Charity; work of mercy. 2. Anything given gratuitously to relieve the poor; a gift of charity." p. 22, Webster's Secondary-School Dictionary, G & C Merriam Company, American Book Company, Springfield, MA, 1913

[256] Statement sworn before John F. Keeley, Notary Public, New York County, NY, Pension file no. 925721, Walter R. Weichert, Record Group 15, National Archives Building, Washington, DC

February 7, 1923 - Viola R. Weichert submitted the following sworn affidavit:[257]

"In answer to paragraphs 1, 2, 3 and 4, I Viola R. Weichert, 331 East 65th St. wish to state that since Nov. 2, 1908, I have owned no property real or personal, stocks, bonds or any other investments, also no interest in property of any kind.

My earning capacity during the year of 1919 and 1920 was far from being sufficient to support myself and three children, owing to the fact that during the whole year of 1919 I was under treatment at the Womans [sic] hospital and at the Neurologic Hospital, Lexington Ave & 67th St N.Y.C. for nervous break down. In the summer of that year I was sent away to St Andrew's convalescent home, Woodcliffe Lake, N.J. to be built up sufficiently strong enough for a severe operation which took place Sept. 18, 1919[.] after three weeks in the Woman's hospital 109th St. I was sent to Burk[e]'s Foundation to convalesce until Nov. 15th. During the years 1917 to the end of 1920 I was obliged to receive relief from the fund of the Spanish War Veterans as my earnings as a clerical worker were not steady and sufficient to supply the needs of the children. I have just recently completed payments on a debt of $150. on account of illness.

Signed Viola R. Weichert"

April 28, 1923 – The Commissioner of Pensions notified Congressman Robsion "that the evidence filed in support of this claim is now being considered by the Board of Review for final settlement, and you and the claimant will be promptly advised of the result."[258]

May 4, 1923 – The United States Pension Office authorized a revised pension for Mrs. Weichert:
Retroactive amount of $12.00 per month from November 2, 1918

---

[257] Statement sworn before John F. Keeley, Notary Public, New York County, NY, Pension file no. 925721, Walter R. Weichert, Record Group 15, National Archives Building, Washington, DC
[258] Pension file no. 925721, Walter R. Weichert, Record Group 15, National Archives Building, Washington, DC

then, forward from September 1, 1922 in the amount of $20.00 per month and $2.00 & $4.00 for three minors.[259]

    For nearly 15 years Mrs. Viola Weichert pleaded with the federal bureaucracy to receive a pension to help support herself and her children. Despite her burdens and the repeated rejections of her applications for pension, Viola Weichert's letters to heads of government agencies and members of Congress were ever cordial. She was skilled with the written word and had good penmanship. Her perseverance eventually succeed; however, her health suffered greatly as a result. The 187-page pension file at the National Archives and Records Administration is documentary evidence of her exhaustive struggle.

---

[259] Certificate No. 925721, Pension file no. 925721, Walter R. Weichert, Record Group 15, National Archives Building, Washington, DC

The Weichert Family Without Walter

The April 1910 United States Census stated that Viola Weichert's daughters Helena,[260] age 6 and Viola,[261] age 2, had been placed in St. Francis Orphan Asylum in West Hoboken (now Union City), New Jersey. Her son, Robert, age 3, remained at home with his mother who was 27 years old.[262] The family was reunited at their home in New York City by 1920.[263]

Walter and Viola Weichert's son, Robert Lawrence Weichert graduated from New York University as a Civil Engineer and for many years was employed by the Bridge Division, State of Vermont. Robert's daughter Lucille Weichert Croscup described her dad as "a good father, very intellectual (IQ 150+), very stoic and not a worrier." Despite not being a physical individual, Robert took his love for photography to the top of the George Washington Bridge to photograph it through its cables. He had no fear of heights. She said that her father understood the meaning of the expression, "when your number's up..." He was of the understanding that his father had been born in Basel, Switzerland. Robert L. Weichert passed away on October 31, 1983.

Robert L. Weichert was only 18 months old when his father was murdered on board the collier *Abarenda*. What Robert knew about his father may have been told to him years later by his mother. Lucille Weichert Croscup, daughter of Robert and Eleanor (nee Bergeron) Weichert, recalled in May 2012 having

---

[260] Year: 1910; Census Place: West Hoboken Ward 2, Hudson, New Jersey; Roll: T624_894; p. 18A; Enumeration District: 0285; FHL microfilm: 1374907
[261] Year: 1910; Census Place: West Hoboken Ward 2, Hudson, New Jersey; Roll: T624_894; p. 17B; Enumeration District: 0285; FHL microfilm: 1374907
[262] Year: 1910; Census Place: Jersey City Ward 12, Hudson, New Jersey; Roll: T624_893; p. 16B; Enumeration District: 0226; Image: 513; FHL Number: 1374906.
[263] Year: 1920; Census Place: Manhattan Assembly District 14, New York, New York; Roll: T625_1210; Page: 6A; Enumeration District: 1013; Image: 1051

been told that, "My grandfather Walter Weichert was an officer on a naval ship (I don't know the name.). His cap was very similar to the captain's cap. He was coming up a ladder when a sailor who had been thrown in the brig by the captain saw him. Thinking that he was the captain, he took an axe and decapitated him. Afterwards, he apologized because it was a case of mistaken identity. He said he had nothing against my grandfather. It was the captain he despised."[264]

In 1927, both, 22 year old Helena Weichert and her 19 year old sister Viola Weichert appeared in separate newspaper advertisements, each for *"Black and White Cold Cream"*. The single-column ads featured a headshot photograph of one of the young ladies. Perhaps due to her darker complexion, Helena's *"Blanco y Negro"* ads were in Spanish in southwest U.S. newspapers such as *La Prensa* in San Antonio, Texas.[265] Viola sported a bobbed haircut in her photo with the opening line, "Just like Peter Pan refused to grow up, I'm going to refuse to grow old…"[266] Each advertisement featuring the sisters included their actual home address in New York City.

Viola Ruth (nee Weichert) Ward was a very religious person. She was very fond of classical music, especially compositions by Antonio Vivaldi. She and her husband, James had three sons, James, Robert and Thomas.[267] Viola Ward passed away at the age of 101 on March 6, 2009.[268]

---

[264] Recollection of Lucille Weichert Croscup concerning the murder of her Grandfather, Walter R. Weichert. Provided to the author May 2012
[265] Helena Weichert in *Blanco y Negro (Black and White Cold Cream)* advertisement, *La Prensa*, March 3, 1927, San Antonio, TX, p. 7
[266] Viola Weichert in Black and White Cold Cream advertisement, *Joplin Globe*, March 15, 1927, Joplin, MO, p. 5
[267] Conversation with Lucille Weichert Croscup, niece of Viola Ruth (nee Weichert) Ward, 2016
[268] Social Security Death Index

Helena Mary Weichert was an avid reader and a logical thinker. She enjoyed pictures of scenery. She was very creative, but always desired to be more creative. As Mrs. Rodriguez, she had two daughters, Didi and Elena.[269] She passed away on January 9, 1995.[270]

Viola Ruth (nee Patterson) Weichert remarried sometime between 1930 and 1940 to Joseph R. Rampfeil. At one time, Viola's daughter Helena lived with them in Queens, New York. Her granddaughter Lucille Weichert Croscup recalled that she was always excited to see her "Nana" and respected her. She described her as very intelligent and refined; a classy lady with a stately appearance who had good taste. Viola was not a woman of means. As evidenced by the many letters she wrote during her plight to secure a pension following her first husband's death, her penmanship was beautiful. She enjoyed an occasional drink, her preference was *Manhattans* and was a chain smoker of *Chesterfield* cigarettes. She passed away in Clinton Corners, New York at the age of 90.[271]

---

[269] Conversation with Lucille Weichert Croscup, niece of Helena Mary Weichert May 2016
[270] Social Security Death Index
[271] Conversation with Lucille Weichert Croscup, Granddaughter of Viola Ruth (nee Patterson) Weichert, later Rampfeil, May 2016

Chief Officer Walter Robert Weichert's Final Rest

Chief Officer Walter R. Weichert was originally interred in the "Naval Graveyard" outside of San Juan, Porto Rico.[272] A change of name of the cemetery likely took place as the official U.S. Navy *burial* register stated that his place of burial was in grave 204 of the "San Juan Military Cemetery".[273] The cemetery in which Chief Officer[274] Walter R. Weichert was interred was later renamed Fort Brooke[275] Post Cemetery.[276]

Nearly 52 years after his interment, Chief Officer Walter R. Weichert's remains were disinterred from Grave 132, Section A, Ft. Brooke Military Cemetery and reinterred at the Puerto Rico National Cemetery, Bayamon, P.R., on January 14, 1960, in Section C, Grave 544. His casket was buried in a grave five feet deep. A vault was not used. The emblem on his stone marker was

---

[272] Log of the United States Naval Auxiliary *Abarenda*, Record Group 24; National Archives Bldg., Washington, DC

[273] Register of Dead, Naval Hospital, San Juan, PR, p. 3, Record Group 52; National Archives Bldg., Washington, DC

[274] Burial records of the Veterans Administration state Weichert's grade as "Chief Officer"

[275] The identification of the Fort Brooks Post Cemetery on that National Archives held document was most likely in error. It should have been labeled Fort Brooke. A page inside the bound volume contains the correct identification of the cemetery. Official Record of Interments in the Post Cemetery, Fort Brooks, P.R. (Originally identified as: Supplemental Vol. Accession N3-15-86-4, RG 94, Entry 627) Record Group 92, Vol. 92, NM-81/A-1 Entry 627, HM 2008, National Archives Bldg., Washington, DC

[276] "On October 18th, the American forces under Gen. John R. Brooke took formal possession of Puerto Rico." The San Juan Military Reservation, established in 1898, was officially designated in 1943 as "Fort Brooke in honor of Major General Brooke, who was the island's first American governor." Reading 3: The Commonwealth of Puerto Rico, National Park Service, website, http://www.nps.gov/nr/twhp/wwwlps/lessons/60sanjuan/60facts3.htm

Christian.[277] The stone marker was ordered from the Columbus Marble Works, Columbus, Mississippi, on May 6, 1960.[278]

The author paid his respects at Chief Officer Weichert's grave in the Puerto Rico National Cemetery, Bayamon, Puerto Rico, on December 26, 2013. He placed on the grave, a small article provided to him by Lucille Weichert Croscup, Walter R. Weichert's Granddaughter.

Weichert's grave site is in one of the older sections of the well-groomed cemetery; just few steps from the southern edge of the cemetery. The grounds beyond his grave are still in their natural, forested state that provide a cool morning shade against the strong tropical sun.

---

[277] Record of Interment, Department of the Army (DA) Form 2122, Dated February 3, 1960, signed by Carlos Garcia Curbelo. Superintendent, Puerto Rico National Cemetery, Record Group 92. The National Archives at College Park, College Park, Maryland

[278] Report of Interment, (unsigned), Quartermaster Corps (QMC) Form 14, Record Group 92. The National Archives at College Park, College Park, Maryland

More Tragedies in the Life of Viola Weichert

Tragedies befell Viola Ruth (nee Patterson) Weichert's family long before she reached adulthood. Born on August 25, 1878, she was no stranger to adversity. Her mother "Katie" Catherine (nee Healy) Patterson was born in 1858[279] in New Orleans, Louisiana to Mary and Andrew Healy who immigrated from Ireland.[280] Viola Weichert's father, Robert L. Patterson, was born in New Orleans, Louisiana (about) 1856[281]. Robert's mother Ruth Ann (nee Golden) was from Pennsylvania, born about 1823.[282] His Father, Ebenezer Angus Patterson was born in New York (about) 1815. They were married in Philadelphia, Pennsylvania on October 22, 1837.[283]

Mother Passed On

On February 7, 1877, Catherine Healy married Robert L. Patterson.[284] Robert had been in publishing much of his life, starting as an apprentice printer[285] and later became one of the

---

[279] Certificate of Death State of Louisiana, Secretary of State, Division of Archives, Records Management, and History. *Vital Records Indices*. Baton Rouge, LA, USA.

[280] Tenth Census of the United States, 1880. (NARA microfilm publication T9, 1,454 rolls). Records of the Bureau of the Census, Record Group 29. National Archives, Washington, D.C.

[281] 1870 U.S. census, population schedules. NARA microfilm publication M593, 1,761 rolls. Washington, D.C.: National Archives and Records Administration.

[282] 1870 U.S. census, population schedules. NARA microfilm publication M593, 1,761 rolls. Washington, D.C.: National Archives and Records Administration.

[283] Pennsylvania and New Jersey, Church and Town Records, 708-1985, Historical Society of Pennsylvania, Reel 387

[284] State of Louisiana, Secretary of State, Division of Archives, Records Management, and History. *Vital Records Indices*. Baton Rouge, LA, USA.

[285] 1870 U.S. census, population schedules. NARA microfilm publication M593, Washington, D.C.: National Archives and Records Administration.

publishers of the New Orleans newspaper, *The Daily Truth*.[286] Catherine Patterson died at the age of 34 on September 5, 1892 from tuberculosis (phthisis pulmonalis).[287] Robert L. Patterson married his second wife, Mary Angela[288] Gaines on April 12, 1893.[289] His 26 year old bride was born in Mexico and immigrated to the United States in 1892.[290]

Death of Father

Although a good husband, Patterson was unsuccessful in business and was hard pressed to support his large family. Robert Patterson was "passionately fond of base ball" [sic] as was Homer Bird, "a prosperous contractor" of New Orleans, Louisiana. Bird was a prominent member of the Merchants Dealers and Lumbermen's Exchange. Bird and Patterson had become "acquainted at the ball grounds and often met there." They were members of the base ball *Rooters Club*.[291]

In 1896, Homer Bird stood in front of the Merchants Dealers and Lumbermen's Exchange of New Orleans[292] where he caught "a meaningful glance from Norma Strong and followed her." Norma Strong was described as "beautiful, of medium height, with a charming figure - one of those who easily turn the

---

[286] *Chronicling America*, Library of Congress, website, http://chroniclingamerica.loc.gov/lccn/sn88064699/
[287] Certificate of Death State of Louisiana, Secretary of State, Division of Archives, Records Management, and History. *Vital Records Indices*. Baton Rouge, LA
[288] Twelfth Census of the United States, 1900. Washington, D.C.: National Archives and Records Administration, 1900. T623
[289] Marriage License, State of Louisiana, Secretary of State, Division of Archives, Records Management, and History. Vital Records Indices. Baton Rouge, LA
[290] Twelfth Census of the United States, 1900. National Archives and Records Administration, Washington, D.C., T623
[291] Murder in Klondike, *The Saint Paul Globe*, Saint Paul, MN, July 30, 1899, p. 8
[292] The Wages of Jealousy, *The Amenia Times*, Amenia New York, December 23, 1899

heads of men of weak moral nature." Later, he "installed the woman in a cottage on Hagan Street."[293]

The Alaskan *Gold Rush* began in August 1896, "With cries of "Gold! Gold! in the Klondike!""[294] Robert L. Patterson planned an expedition to the Klondike and shared his scheme with Homer Bird.[295] It's believed that Norma Strong "persuaded Bird to go on an expedition to the Klondike" to take him from his family then "throw him over should she captivate a richer man in the gold fields."[296] Other members of the Patterson expedition were a 26 year old bookkeeper named Hans Hurlin; printer Charles Scheffler, age 27; Homer Bird and Norma Strong. Only Bird knew that Strong would participate and join the group in San Francisco.[297]

The tragic tale of the expedition was revealed through the testimony of Naomi Strong, heretofore known as Norma Strong, one of the witnesses for the prosecution of Homer Bird. Edits to the court's narrative herein replace the term "plaintiff in error" with the name "Homer Bird." The tabloids across the country published various accounts of the events of the excursion and murders of Hurlin and Patterson, some more graphic and sensational than others.

---

[293] Murder in Klondike, *The Saint Paul Globe*, Saint Paul, MN, July 30, 1899, p. 8
[294] Klondike Gold Rush, National Historical Park, Alaska, National Park Service website, http://www.nps.gov/klgo/learn/goldrush.htm
[295] The Wages of Jealousy, *The Amenia Times*, Amenia New York, December 23, 1899
[296] Murder in Klondike, *The Saint Paul Globe*, Saint Paul, MN, July 30, 1899, p. 8
[297] The Wages of Jealousy, *The Amenia Times*, Amenia New York, December 23, 1899

The court record provided the most objective description of the events. The following excerpts from the transcript of the first trial of Homer Bird in 1899:

"In the spring of 1898," Homer Bird, "Hurlin, the deceased, Charles Scheffler, R. L. Patterson, and Naomi Strong organized a party to prospect in Alaska for gold. Each of the men was to contribute five hundred dollars for purchasing an outfit. Scheffler failed with his contribution, and plaintiff in error furnished something over one thousand dollars. At San Francisco, California, a small steam launch and a scow thirty-two feet long by six feet beam were bought, together with the usual supply of food, clothing, etc.

Naomi Strong "was designated on the indictment by the name of Naomi Strong. It was contended that Naomi Strong was not her name, and" Homer Bird "objected to her testimony on the ground that her true name had not been furnished on the list of witnesses given. The objection was overruled, and the ruling was assigned as error. At the request of" Homer Bird, "the jury was withdrawn and the witness examined before the court as to her name, and she testified that her maiden name was Naomi Strong, but she had been married and divorced. She refused to give the name of her husband. She also testified that she had been divorced ten or twelve years, and upon her divorce she went by her maiden name. Subsequently she went by the name of Byers, when living with a man by that name, and, after meeting" Homer Bird, she went by his name. She testified that she met" Homer Bird "in 1893 or 1894, and left New Orleans with him the first of May, 1898, to join the expedition to Alaska during which the homicide was committed. She and" Homer Bird "traveled as husband and wife under the name of Mr. and Mrs. Bundick."

"The party sailed from San Francisco, and reached St. Michael July 4. Shortly after, they started up the Yukon River, reaching a point in September about six hundred miles above its mouth, and there determined to go into winter quarters, and for

101

that purpose began the construction of a cabin. Dissentions arose in the party..." "A resolution to separate was formed, but its execution was postponed at the request of" Homer Bird "until the cabin should be finished. The cabin was finished on September 26 [1898]. In the meantime, there had been disagreements as to the division of supplies."

"...on the morning of the 27th of September [1898]" "the party collected for breakfast" "on that morning -- Patterson, Hurlin, and Scheffler going first," Homer Bird "subsequently joining them, he seating himself on his bunk back of the others, and they sat as follows: Patterson on the right, Scheffler in the center, and Hurlin on the left." According to Naomi Strong, "Scheffler and I were talking about a trap I had set to catch some grouse, and _____ ... A. _____ we were talking about it, and all at once I heard Mr. Bird's gun click -- shotgun -- when he broke it, it clicked, of course, and I looked up, and he had the gun to his shoulder, and in the meantime Mr. Scheffler looked around; I think he fired at Mr. Hurlin, and then Scheffier looked around and held up his hands and told him for God's sake not to shoot him, and I jumped up after he fired at Hurlin, and Mr. Patterson kind of jumped back of me -- jumped behind me like, and I asked Bird not to shoot; he had the gun to his shoulder all the time, and I jumped and run; put my head over Patterson's shoulder and run through the boat, and just as I passed him in the boat, he fired at Mr. Patterson, and Patterson jumped overboard; whether the shot struck him when he jumped overboard I don't know, and in the meantime I jumps out on the beach, and Mr. Patterson jumps overboard, and Mr. Bird comes running out, climbs over the bow of the boat with two guns in his hand -- his own and Mr. Scheffler's -- and heads Patterson off; the boat was in the water just kind of half on the beach and half in the water, and so Mr. Patterson wades around on the side of the boat to get out, and Bird heads him off and tells him not to come near him, and Patterson kept begging him not to shoot him, and Bird up with his gun again says, 'Bob, you dirty son of a bitch, you're the cause of this,' and shot at him the second time, and Patterson came to the beach."

"Q. Well, compose yourself, Mrs. Strong, if you can, and go on and state what occurred there. What happened when Mr. Patterson got to the beach?"
"A. They were all on the beach then, and he begged Bird not to shoot him."

"Q. What did he say to him?"
"A. He held out his hands and told him for God's sake to think of his poor family."

"Q. What did Bird say?"
"A. I don't remember any more what he did say; I think he says, 'Bob, I have thought of our families,' or something like that."

"Q. At the time he fired at Hurlin, did you see what Mr. Hurlin did? Immediately after, as far as Hurlin was concerned? Immediately after the shooting of Hurlin, what followed [witness sobs]; what did he do, Mrs. Strong?"

"A. Mr. Hurlin?"
"Q. Yes."

"A. He never moved at all; he sat in the same position when he was shot."
"Q. Did his body change position at all?"

"A. No; just remained that way for quite a while."

"Q. Did you see any evidence of a wound on Mr. Hurlin -- anything?"

103

"A. I saw where there was a hole in his head right here, the left side."[298]

Robert L. Patterson died of his wounds on April 8, 1899 at Anvik, Alaska.[299] "A good husband, he went in search of gold that he might better support his wife, his second, and his large family by both wives. Since his departure one trouble after another has pressed upon his wife and children. They are now in absolute want."[300]

Homer Bird on Trial

The October 3, 1899 arrest of Homer Bird for the murders Robert L. Patterson and Hans Hurlin is documented in the following correspondence from James M. Shoup, U.S. Marshal to the Attorney General of the United States (John William Griggs[301]). His incarceration and execution were recorded in his prison file.

Bird was tried in 1899 and convicted of murder and sentenced to be hanged. "This is the first verdict of murder in the first degree rendered in Alaska."[302] The United States Supreme Court granted Bird a new trial. He was again put on trial in 1901 and was once more convicted. Again there was an appeal on a

---

[298] U.S. Supreme Court, Bird v. United States, 187 U.S. 118 (1902), Bird v. United States, No. 306, Argued October 14, 1902, Decided November 17, 1902, 187 U.S. 118, Error to the District Court of the United States for the District of Alaska
[299] "From Sitka's Past", Alaska State Library, Juneau, AK
[300] Murder in Klondike, *The Saint Paul Globe*, Saint Paul, MN, July 30, 1899, p. 8
[301] John William Griggs, Forty-Third Attorney General 1898-1901, The United States Department of Justice, website, http://www.justice.gov/ag/bio/griggs-john-william
[302] Homer Bird, The assassin of Patterson and Hurlin, Will Die, *The Daily Picayune*, December 14, 1899, p. 8

writ or error, and a third trial was granted by the courts. Bird was tried for the third time in 1902 and convicted of murder. No further appeals were granted. Throughout the lengthy process Mrs. Bird traveled extensively and contacted officials up through the highest levels in Washington on behalf of her husband. President McKinley when the first respite was granted and near the end sought help from President Theodore Roosevelt, Attorney General Knox and others with whom she met. The "convincing evidence of her husband's guilt and the atrocity of the crime made it out of the question for any further clemency to be exercised."[303]

"Sitka, Alaska, October 31, 1899.[304]

The Attorney General,
    Washington, D.C.

Sir,
I have the honor to say that during the night of September 30th, A.H. Bird held for a double murder in the U.S. jail at St. Michael, Alaska, escaped therefrom by exiting through the floor with a saw made from an ordinary case knife which he managed some way to procure. The crime committed by Bird is one of the most heinous and inexcusable in the annals of crime. There were four detained witnesses held at the expense of the Government in his case. U.S. Deputy Marshal Vawter was about to depart with Bird on the U.S. Revenue Cutter Bear for Sitka. Navigation was about to close for the season and it is evident that unless Bird was speedily recaptured he could not be tried before August of next year The great hardship that this would impose upon the witnesses, besides

---

[303] Homer Bird / The Alaskan Murderer Will Be Executed Tomorrow, *Daily Albuquerque Citizen*, Albuquerque, NM, March 5, 1903, p. 1
[304] Letter, dated October 31, 1899, from James M. Shoup, U.S. Marshal, to U.S. Attorney General. Alaska State Archives

the great expense to the Government, induced Deputy Vawter to offer a personal reward for his recapture, and to employ possemen to assist him in the search. Bird was taken on the evening of October 3rd by Indians on an Island adjacent to St. Michael, and Deputy Vawter paid the reward; he also paid the possemen, and has vouchers in duplicate for both payments. I am of the opinion that Deputy Vawter cannot be reimbursed through this office, but I think that it is a meritorious case, and that he should either be paid under the provisions of Sec. 84C R.S: the apprehension Travelling and Miscellaneous Expenses. when approved by the Attorney General, page 1114, Statutes at large-1898-1899; the fund Fines and Forfeitures for Alaska, or a special act of Congress.

Very respectfully,
James M. Shoup [signed]
U.S. Marshal"

Table 1 – Prison Record of Homer Bird, U.S. Jail, Sitka, Alaska [305]

DATE	PAGE / LINE NUMBER	COMMITTED	BY WHOM COMMITTED	OFFENCE	DISCHARGED	RECEIVED AT SITKA	SENTENCE	EXPIRATION
OCT 1899	48 / 57	JUN 27, 1899	L.B. Shepherd, Commissioner	Murder	///add detained witnesses///	OCT 23, 1899	Awaiting Trial	

[305] Jail Register for the U.S. Jail in Sitka, Alaska, Alaska State Archives

NOV 1900	OCT 1900	SEP 1900	AUG 1900					DEC 1899
102 / 1	/ 2	93 / 2	88 / 2	/ 4	/ 4	/ 7	/ 14	57 / 39
DEC 13, 1899	DEC 13, 1899	DEC 13, 1899	DEC 13, 1899	DEC 13, 1899	DEC 13, 1899	DEC 13, 1899	DEC 13, 1899	DEC 13, 1899
District Court	District Court	District Court	District Court	District Court	District Court	District Court	District Court	District Court
Murder	Murder	Murder	Murder	Murder	Murder	Murder	Murder	Murder
DEC 17, 1899	DEC 17, 1899	DEC 17, 1899				DEC 17, 1899	DEC 17, 1899	DEC 17, 1899
								To be executed at Sitka FEB 9, 1900

SEP 1901	AUG 1901	JUL 1901	MAY 1901	MAR 1901	FEB 1901	JAN 1901	DEC 1900
148 / 12	/ 14	141 / 26	135 / 68	121 / 1	116 / 1	112 / 1	107 / 1
DEC 13, 1899	DEC 13, 1899	DEC 13, 1899	DEC 13, 1899	DEC 13, 1899	DEC 13, 1899	DEC 13, 1899	DEC 13, 1899
District Court	District Court	District Court	District Court	District Court	District Court	District Court	District Court
Murder	Murder	Murder	Murder	Murder	Murder	Murder	Murder
Transferred to Skagway Sept 30, 1901			Charge no board for 31st				
May 31, 1901	May 31, 1901	May 31, 1901	May 31, 1901	DEC 17, 1899	DEC 17, 1899	DEC 17, 1899	DEC 17, 1899
Awaiting Trial	Awaiting Trial	Awaiting Trial	Awaiting Trial				

JUL 1902	JUN 1902	MAY 1902	APR 1902	MAR 1902	FEB 1902	JAN 1902
/ 4	201 / 5	/ 10	192 / 18	/ 31	/ 47	/ 92
JAN 16, 1902	JAN 16, 1902	JAN 16, 1902	JAN 16, 1902	JAN 16, 1902	JAN 16, 1902	JAN 16, 1902
U.S. District Court	U.S. District Court	U.S. District Court	U.S. District Court	U.S. District Court	U.S. District Court	U.S. District Court
Murder	Murder	Murder	Murder	Murder	Murder	Murder
				Stay of Proceedings Issued Mar 13, 1902		
JAN 22, 1902	JAN 22, 1902	JAN 22, 1902	JAN 22, 1902	JAN 22, 1902	JAN 22, 1902	JAN 22, 1902
Awaiting Trial	Awaiting Trial	Awaiting Trial	Awaiting Trial	Death	Death	Death
					Apr 11, 19___	Apr 11

109

JAN 1903	DEC 1902	NOV 1902	OCT 1902	SEP 1902	AUG 1902
231 / 1	226 / 1	221 / 1	216 / 1	212 / 1	209 / 3
JAN 6, 1902	JAN 6, 1902	JAN 6, 1902	JAN 16, 1902	JAN 16, 1902	JAN 16, 1902
U.S. District Court	U.S. District Court	U.S. District Court	U.S. District Court	U.S. District Court	U.S. District Court
Murder	Murder	Murder	Murder	Murder	Murder
JAN 22, 1902	JAN 22, 1902	JAN 22, 1902	JAN 22, 1902	JAN 22, 1902	JAN 22, 1902
Death	Awaiting Sentence	Awaiting Trial	Awaiting Trial	Awaiting Trial	Awaiting Trial
MAR 6, 1903					

FEB 1903	235 / 1	JAN 6, 1903	U.S. District Court	Murder		JAN 22, 1902	Death	MAR 6, 1903
MAR 1903	239 / 1		U.S. District Court	Murder	Executed MAR 6, 1903	JAN 22, 1902	Death	MAR 6, 1903

Justice

March 6, 1903, Sitka, Alaska, Homer Bird was taken from his cell at 1:00 p.m. "He walked to the gallows with great composure. To the last moment he protested his innocence. From the gallows he made a short speech, saying that a great wrong was about to be done in taking his life and that he was absolutely guiltless." "He did not show the least nervousness when the cap was put on his head and the rope adjusted about his throat." At 1:40 p.m. "the drop was sprung which sent the condemned murderer to eternity. His neck was broken in the fall and death quickly ensued."[306]

---

[306] Homer Bird Suffered the Death Penalty for His Crime, *The Daily Picayune*, New Orleans, LA, March 10, 1903, p. 1

A History of the U.S.S. *Abarenda*

Born in England

Prior to her collier (coal transport) service in support of the United States Navy, the steamship *Abarenda* was a commercial freighter based in the United Kingdom. *Abarenda* was constructed by Edwards Shipbuilding Company, Limited, for the Graham Steamship Company, Limited, which operated her from 1892 to 1898.

The freighter's launching was reported in the British shipbuilding trade journal, *Iron*: "Abarenda. - On August 11, [1892] Messrs. Edwards' Shipbuilding Company, Limited, of Howdon-on-Tyne, launched a steel screw-steamer, built to the order of Messrs. James Graham & Co., of Newcastle-on-Tyne. Dimensions: - Length over all, 326 feet; breadth extreme, 42 feet; depth, moulded, [sic] 28 ½ feet. Deadweight capacity, 4,700 tons. Engines and boilers by Messrs. Hawthorne, Leslie & Co., Limited, of St. Peter's, Newcastle-on-Tyne. Engine cylinders, 23, 38, and 62 inches, by 42-inch stroke. The speed expected to be obtained is 10 knots."[307]

Table 2 – S.S. *Abarenda* - Specifications as documented in the British Registry in 1892[308]

Official Number	101805
Name of Ship	Abarenda
Signal Letters	M.T.F.G.
No., Date, and Port of Registry	24 in 1892. Newcastle

---

[307] Naval Architecture, Launches, English; *Iron*, No, 1,023. Vol. XL., August 19, 1892, London, U.K., p. 168
[308] Certificate of British Registry – Form No. 9 and Transcript of Register for Transmission to Registrar - General of shipping and Seamen - Form No. 19; Records of the Registrar General of Shipping and Seamen and successor, BT 110/1/2, Ship *Abarenda*; The National Archives of the United Kingdom

No., Date, and Port of Previous Registry	First Registry
Whether British or Foreign Built	British
Whether a Sailing or Steam Ship; and if a Steam Ship, how propelled	Steam, Screw
Where Built	Howdon
When Built	1892
Name and Address of Builders	Edwards Shipbuilding Company, Limited, Howdon on Tyne
Number of Decks	2
Number of Masts	2
Rigged	Schooner
Stern	Elliptic
Build	Clincher
Galleries	none
Head	none
Framework and description of vessel	Steel
Number of Bulkheads	6
Number of water ballast tanks and their capacity in tons	6	487 tons
Length from fore part of stem, under the bowsprit, to the aft side of the head of the stern post	314 ft.
Length at quarter of depth from top of weather deck at side amidships to bottom of keel	314 ft.
Main breadth to outside of plank	42 ft.
Depth in hold from tonnage depth to ceiling at amidships	26 ft.
Depth from top of beam amidships to top of keel	29.3 ft.
Depth from top of deck at side amidships to bottom of keel	30.1 ft.
Round of beam	0.75 ft.
Length of engine room, if any	42 ft.
Particulars of Displacement	
Total to quarter the depth from weather deck at side amidships to bottom of keel	6515 tons
Ditto per inch immersion at same depth	28 tons

Particulars of Engines	Number of engines	3
	Engines description	Triple Expansion[309]
	When made	1892

---

[309] The engine was later described as vertical triple expansion, single screw. Register of Ships, Bureau of Steam Engineering, *Annual Reports of the Navy Department for the Fiscal Year 1908*, Government Printing Office, Washington, D.C., 1908, p. 702

	Number of Cylinders	3
	Diameter of Cylinders	23", 38", 62"
	Length of Stroke	42"
	N.H.P.	250
	I.H.P.	1250
	Speed of Ship	9 Knots
	Name and address of makers:	Hawthorn Leslie & Co., Ltd., Newcastle on Tyne
Boilers	Number	2
	Iron or steel	Steel
	Pressure when loaded	160 lbs.
	When made	1892
	Name and address of makers	Hawthorn Leslie & Co., Ltd., Newcastle on Tyne

Particulars of Tonnage	
Gross tonnage	
Under Tonnage Deck	2902.56 tons
Closed in spaces under Tonnage Deck if (any):	
Space or spaces between decks	
Poop	83.63 tons
Forecastle	5.04 tons
Deck houses	50.62 tons
Other closed in spaces, if any, as follows	
Chart House	5.05 tons
Excess of Hatchways	28.74 tons
Spaces for machinery, light and air	47.81 tons
Deductions Allowed	
On account of space required for propelling power	999.50 tons
On account of space occupied by Seamen or Apprentices, and appropriated for their use, and kept free from Goods, or Stores of every kind, not being the personal property of the Crew	81.47 tons
These spaces are the following, viz:	
Boatswains' stores	17.52 tons
Master's berth	10.65 tons
Chart room	5.05 tons
Total deductions	1114.19 tons

Gross tonnage	3123.45 tons	8839.36 cubic metres
Deductions as per contra	1114.19	3153.16 cubic metres
Registered tonnage	2009.26	5686.20 cubic metres

Master: Robert Macgregor, Certificate of Competency no. 90189
Owner: The Graham Steamship Company, Limited having its principal place of business at Gails' Buildings in the City of Newcastle on Tyne
Dated at Newcastle: 12th day of October 1892

Seven days after being recorded with the Registrar General of Shipping and Seamen, the freighter S.S. *Abarenda* steamed from the Albert Edward Dock[310] at North Shields on the Tyne River for her trial run on October 19, 1892. She "had a successful trial trip, when a mean speed of 10¾ knots was obtained."[311]

Freighter Abarenda

S.S. *Abarenda's* departure from the port of Shields later on October 19th, en route to Galveston, Texas marked the beginning of her commercial operation for The Graham Steamship Company.[312] On her return cruise she carried American cotton bound for Liverpool.[313] Details concerning her cargoes of cotton were reported the following year, "… the S.S. Abarenda, of 3,123 tons has just loaded for Liverpool with 9,200 bales of cotton - the

---

[310] Late Shipping News; *The Shields Daily Gazette and Shipping Telegraph*, October 20, 1892, North Shields / South Shields, United Kingdom, p. 3
[311] Launches and Trial Trips, *The Marine Engineer*, Vol. XIV, November 1, 1892, London, United Kingdom, p. 385
[312] Mercantile Shipping News, *The Standard*, October 20, 1892, London, United Kingdom, p. 8
[313] The American Cotton Market, *Manchester Evening News*, December 24, 1892, Greater Manchester, United Kingdom, p. 3

largest cargo yet shipped, - and has crossed the bar drawing 282 feet of water!"[314]

Although S.S. *Abarenda* was registered following her construction in 1892 as a steam vessel, she employed at least two sails in 1894. That and several other architectural details appeared in a newspaper account of a "terrible voyage" during which she was "at mercy of wind and wave". *Abarenda* departed her home port on the Tyne, Sunday, February 18, 1894, carrying "900 tons of bunker coals and 800 tons of ballast." Her destination was Baltimore, Maryland. On the morning of the following Sunday she was struck by heavy seas off the northern coast of Scotland, "which laid about 50 feet of her forward bulwarks flat on the deck." Her "after flying bridge was carried away". The 1 3/8 inch iron rods of her steering gear "were snapped like threads." *Abarenda's* "three after cargo booms were brought down, and everything was swept off the poop deck. The bunker coals were shifted, carrying away all stanchions, angle irons, and breaking shifting boards in bunkers, throwing the ship on her beam ends. The tarpaulins on the hatches blown to pieces, and the hatches were blown off and hurled in the holds and into the sea." "Captain Macgregor ordered the mainstay sail set to help bring the steamer's head on. The sail was immediately blown to ribbons." The Captain used oil "which prevented the heavy seas from breaking on board the steamer." Despite the ship's heavy rolling, the crew took advantage of the moderated winds the following day to clear the ship of wreckage, repair the steering gear, trim the ship and "secure the coals and ballast from shifting again." On February 28th a hurricane from the southwest threatened the freighter. Gale force winds as great as 100 miles per hour and seas as high as 40 feet threatened the ship. Oil was used several more

---

[314] *The Shields Daily Gazette and Shipping Telegraph*, November 20, 1893, South Shields, England, United Kingdom, p. 2

times as before with success. "The forestay sail was set to try to get the ship before the wind, which fortunately succeeded, before the sail was blown away." Conditions improved on March 2nd as *Abarenda* was 250 miles off the Irish coast. The ship proceeded to Cape Henry, Virginia without further damage.[315]

Collier *Abarenda*

The Graham Steamship Company's *Abarenda* transported a variety of cargoes between ports of the United Kingdom and United States from 1892 – 1898. S.S. *Abarenda* departed from Cardiff, England on April 6, 1898[316] for her final cruise under the Graham name. Following her arrival at New York on April 27, 1898,[317] she was met by United States Navy examiners her for purchase. The Naval Board on Auxiliary Cruisers had "received instructions from the Navy Department to take steps for securing additions to the fleet of colliers." Negotiations began the preceding day for "the purchase of two first-class English vessels," *Abarenda* and *Regulus*, which were in port at New York. Both vessels were of Newcastle, England registry and would likely be bought by the Navy. *Abarenda* was described in the newspaper report as having "exceptional speed for a vessel of her class."[318]

---

[315] "At Mercy of Wind & Wave", *Sunderland Daily Echo*, April 7, 1894, Sunderland England, United Kingdom, p. 3
[316] Latest Shipping, *Evening Telegraph*, April 8, 1898, Angus, Scotland, United Kingdom, p. 5
[317] Arrivals at Foreign Ports, *The Liverpool Echo*, April 28, 1898, Merseyside, England, United Kingdom, p. 3
[318] "To Purchase More Colliers", *The New York Times*, April 28, 1898, New York, NY

Hand inscribed in red ink upon the Certificate of British Registry[319] for *Abarenda*:

"Custom House Newcastle May 27th 1898.
Registry closed 27 May 1898.
Vessel sold to United States Government as per letter from H.B.M.[320] Consul General at New York.
Per Certificate of Registry Seal 29 May 1898.
[Signed] J. Clark Hall[321] Registrar"

The United States Navy purchased *Abarenda* on May 5, 1898 for $175,000. Her name remained unchanged.[322] *Abarenda* arrived in the East River the next morning and steamed to the entrance of the New York Navy Yard. From there she was towed by navy tug boats and "placed alongside the Cob Dock, forward of the receiving ship Vermont"[323] to await her conversion for collier service.[324] Although *Abarenda's* maximum speed of 9.0 knots was documented in the U.S. Navy file, she achieved 11" 2 knots;

---

[319] Certificate of British Registry - Form No. 9 and Transcript of Register for Transmission to Registrar - General of shipping and Seamen - Form No. 19; Records of the Registrar General of Shipping and Seamen and successor, BT 110/1/2, Ship *Abarenda*; The National Archives of the United Kingdom; Imperial Calendar for 1898 the Registrar General of Shipping and Seamen

[320] Abbreviation H.B.M. - Her Britannic Majesty; *The Universal Cyclopaedia*, Volume 1, D. Appleton and Co., New York, N.Y., 1900, p.7; Reign of Queen Victoria: June 20, 1837 to January 22, 1901; Queen Victoria, A Biography by Sidney Lee, Smith, Elder & Co., London, U.K., 1903, pp. 48, 538-539

[321] Signature of J. Clark Hall verified via email dated January 5, 2013 to author from James Ross, Remote Enquiries Duty Officer, The National Archives of the United Kingdom

[322] Ship's record card, *Abarenda*, Naval History & Heritage Command, Washington Navy Yard, Washington, DC

[323] "Abarenda at the Cob Dock", *The New York Times*, May 7, 1898, New York, NY

[324] ZC File, *Abarenda*, Naval History & Heritage Command, Washington Navy Yard, Washington, DC

1,468 I.H.P. (indicated horsepower) during her trial run documented on May 6, 1898.[325]

The collier *Abarenda* was first placed in commission at New York on May 20, 1898 under the command of Lieutenant Commander M.B. Buford.[326] That same day, four 3-pounder guns were mounted on the ship.[327] (Those guns would later be replaced by four 6-pounders.[328]) During the Spanish American War, the collier transported coal from Lamberts Point, Virginia to the Atlantic Fleet at Santiago de Cuba and Guantanamo, Cuba. Her 1899 service involved the establishment of a coal depot in Samoa. *Abarenda* was placed out of commission on September 5, 1902. Again commissioned on November 3, 1903, she transported coal the Atlantic Fleet and ammunition to the European Squadron. She was placed out of commission at Norfolk, Virginia on February 21, 1905. On that day, her navy personnel were replaced by a civilian complement from the Naval Auxiliary Service (NAS) and she was placed in service under the command of Master J.W. Holmes for collier duty.[329] The vessel had been taken out of commission due to a shortage of naval officers.[330] The *Abarenda* and most of the Navy's other colliers were "officered and manned" on the same plan as merchant vessels under contract between the respective masters and the Navy Department, but the movement to replace these merchant crews with regular naval

---

[325] Transcribed *11" 2 K* exactly as handwritten from *Ships' Information* card, *Abarenda*, Naval History & Heritage Command, Washington Navy Yard, Washington, DC
[326] ZC File, *Abarenda*, Naval History & Heritage Command, Washington Navy Yard, Washington, DC
[327] Ship's Record Card, 1892-1899, *Abarenda*, Naval History & Heritage Command, Washington Navy Yard, Washington, DC
[328] Ship's Information, *Abarenda*, Naval History & Heritage Command, Washington Navy Yard, Washington, DC
[329] Based on two historical summaries by Fay A. Garrett, ZC File, *Abarenda*, Naval History & Heritage Command, Washington Navy Yard, Washington, DC
[330] Statement of Captain J.E. Pillsbury, Assistant to Chief of Bureau of Navigation, Hearings Before the Subcommittee of House Committee on Appropriations, Deficiency Appropriations for 1905 and Prior Years on General Deficiency Bill, Government Printing Office, Washington, DC, February 17, 1905, pp. 75-76

complements has gone forward as fast as the shortage of officers would permit.[331] The NAS was established in 1905 to replace the Collier Service previously organized in 1898.[332]

Abarenda in 1908

Table 3 – *Abarenda* Manning 1908[333]

Master	1
First officer	1
Second officer	1
Third officer	1
Chief engineer	1
First assistant engineer	1
Second assistant engineer	1
Third assistant engineer	1
Electrician	1
Clerk	1
Boatswain	1
Carpenter	1
Quartermaster	3
Seaman	8
Oiler	3
Fireman	6
Coal passer	3
Steward	1
First cook	1
Second cook	1
Messman	1
Cabin boy	1
Total	40

---

[331] Naval Colliers, Message from the President of the United States to the Two Houses of Congress, Government Printing Office, Washington, DC, p. 981
[332] Naval Overseas Transportation and Shipping Control, Bureau of Naval Personnel, NAVPERS 10829, March 1949, p. 15
[333] Excerpted from Complements of Naval Auxiliaries, *Regulations for the Naval Auxiliary Service*, Government Printing Office, Washington, DC, 1907, p. 31

Table 4 – Specifications of United States Naval Auxiliary *Abarenda* in 1908[334]

Displacement		6,705 tons
Dimensions	Length over all	325' 6"
	Beam	42' ½"
	Mean draft loaded	22' 10"
Speed	Loaded	9 knots
	Light	9.5 knots
Coal consumption		21
Capacity	Bunker	813 tons
	Cargo	3,400 tons
Station		Atlantic Fleet

Abarenda remained on collier duty until she was placed out of service on October 6, 1909. Again, placed in service on May 24, 1910 she resumed her collier service, this time as an auxiliary with the Asiatic Fleet. Upon the United States' entry into the World War in 1917, *Abarenda* was placed in commission and her personnel transitioned to the U.S. Naval Reserve Force. *Abarenda* remained on duty with the Asiatic Fleet through early 1926 except for a brief period where she served as a station ship at Samoa.

The United States Navy had planned to sell *Abarenda* on January 9, 1922; however, she was withdrawn from sale on April 14, 1922. Her classification was changed from Collier (AC13) to Auxiliary Miscellaneous (AG14) on July 1, 1924. The order went out on December 23, 1925 that *Abarenda* be sold. She was stricken from the Navy List and placed out of commission on January 21, 1926. That was not the end of the ship's service.

---

[334] List of Ships of the United States Navy, Auxiliaries, Colliers, *Abarenda*; *Register of the Commissioned and Warrant Officers of the United States Navy and Marine Corps*, Navy Department, U.S. Government Printing Office, Washington, DC, January 1, 1908, p. 234

Freighter *Antonio*, then Scrap

S.R. Paterno of Manila, P.I., purchased the ship in the under sealed bid for $32,000 on February 28, 1926.[335] Under her new name, *Antonio*, the freighter was operated by (Vicente Madrigal)[336] Madrigal & Company of Manila[337] until the vessel was broken up in July 1934 in the Philippines.[338] Madrigal & Company would purchase used ships and refit them to suit his shipping company's needs.[339] The freighter was likely given his son's name, Antonio[340], as Vicente Madrigal typically would name his vessels for family members.[341]

Abarenda's Scrap Paper

A considerable collection of information pertaining to the *Abarenda* is preserved within this volume. Unfortunately, a quantity of documents pertaining to the vessel were deemed to be "useless" and were destroyed. A few weeks before his term in office expired, President Grover Cleveland signed into law, on

---

[335] Ship's record card, *Abarenda*, Naval History & Heritage Command, Washington Navy Yard, Washington, DC

[336] Philippine Vessels, *Merchant Vessels of the United States*, Department of Commerce – Bureau of Navigation, U.S. Government Printing Office, Washington, DC, 1926, p. 956

[337] Steamers and Motorships, *Lloyd's Register of Shipping*, London, U.K., 1927

[338] "Single Ship Report for 1101805" (*Abarenda/Antonio*), [Online version, miramarshipindex.org.nz/ *Miramar Ship Index*, R.B. Haworth, Wellington, New Zealand, 2006.]

[339] *Philippine Tycoon, The Biography of an Industrialist, Vicente Madrigal,* by Carlos Quirino, Madrigal Memorial Foundation, Manila, 1987, p. 42

[340] Antonio Madrigal was born June 8, 1918, *Philippine Tycoon, The Biography of an Industrialist, Vicente Madrigal,* by Carlos Quirino, Madrigal Memorial Foundation, Manila, 1987, p. 179

[341] S.S. *Susana* was named for his wife; S.S. *Don Jose* was named for his late father; *Philippine Tycoon, The Biography of an Industrialist, Vicente Madrigal,* by Carlos Quirino, Madrigal Memorial Foundation, Manila, 1987, p. 40

February 16, 1889, "An act to authorize and provide for the disposition of useless papers in the Executive Departments."

"That whenever there shall be in any one of the Executive Departments of the Government an accumulation of files of papers, which are not needed or useful in the transaction of the current business of such Department and have no permanent value or historical interest, it shall be the duty of the head of such Department to submit to Congress a report of that fact, accompanied by a concise statement of the condition and character of such papers." A joint committee of Congress would review and approve the report and "...then it shall be the duty of such head Sale, etc. of the Department to sell as waste paper, or otherwise dispose of such files of papers upon the best obtainable terms after due publication of notice inviting proposals therefor, and receive and pay the proceeds thereof into the Treasury of the United States, and make report thereof to Congress."[342]

One such report, "Disposition of Useless Papers in the Navy Department" was published on April 27, 1926, three months after the *Abarenda* was stricken from the Navy List. The report included accumulations of official files from the Navy and Marine Corps targeted for sale or destruction as waste paper. Among the numerous obsolete items listed were technical and administrative documents pertaining to the *Abarenda*. Files pertaining to other U.S. Navy vessels were also destroyed.

---

[342] Statutes at Large of the United States Of America, From December, 1887, to March, 1889, and Recent Treaties, Postal Conventions, and Executive Proclamations. Session II. Chapter 171, Government Printing Office, Washington, DC, 1889, p. 672

Table 5 - Disposal of *Abarenda* (AC13) Documentation[343]

Document	Justification for Disposal
2 blue prints of main boiler furnaces (undated)	Duplicates; permanent print retained
Letter re inspection of hull, March 31, 1911	Data embodied in permanent report
Letter re inspection held April 12, 1911	"
Letters of September, October and November 1912, and May 1913, re receipt of General Orders, Nos. 96-236	"
Letter re inspection held September 25, 1912	"
Letter re hull report of March 31, 1914	"
Letter re hull report of September 30, 1914	"
Letter re inspection held February 24, 1915	"
Letter re hull report of March 31, 1915	"
Letter re inspection held March 22, 1916	"
Letter re hull report of March 31, 1917	"
Letter re hull report of June 30, 1917	"

When that law was enacted, federal buildings held overwhelming volumes of rolled, trifold and bound documentation. Suitable facilities for long-term safekeeping were typically not available. Poor environmental conditions degraded the paper records. Fires could easily wipe out these repositories. In that era, straight pins were commonly used to fasten papers together prior to the widespread use of staples. Did those no longer needed documents, sold for scrap, hold any information that would be beneficial to future generations?

---

[343] Disposition of Useless Papers in the Navy Department, 69th Congress, House of Representatives Report No. 1016, p. 6

Index

1st Officer, 9, 14, 79, 88
Abarenda, iii, vii, viii, xii, 7, 9, 10, 11, 12, 13, 14, 15, 16, 19, 20, 21, 22, 23, 24, 25, 26, 27, 41, 42, 43, 44, 45, 46, 47, 48, 50, 51, 52, 53, 54, 56, 63, 64, 66, 75, 77, 78, 79, 82, 88, 93, 96, 112, 115, 116, 117, 118, 119, 120, 121, 122, 123, 124
AC13, 121, 124
Adair, John Alfred McDowell
  Congressman, IN, 76, 77, 78
Adverse Report, 78
affidavit, 48, 69, 83, 90, 91
Ainsworth, F.C., 58, 60
Alexander, 6, 13, 19, 24, 32, 33, 35, 40, 52, 55, 64, 66, 69
Antonio, 94, 122
Anvik, Alaska, 104
Asiatic Fleet, 121
assault, 35, 38, 43, 44, 45, 46
Atlantic Fleet, 119, 121
axe, 14, 16, 18, 19, 20, 21, 33, 34, 35, 94
Baltimore, Maryland, 9
Barnes, Hunter
  Seaman, 11
Barnes, T.H., 24, 43, 44, 48, 49, 51, 52, 53
  Seaman, 43
Barr, Ella, 3
Barr, George W., 3

Barr, Cella, 2
Barry, Edward B., Captain, USN
  Supervisor of Naval Auxiliaries, 1, 7
Basel, Switzerland, 93
Becker, Paul, 62, 69
Beebe, H B.
  Third Assistant Engineer, *Abarenda*, 24
Bell, J. A. Bell, Commander, U.S. Navy, Retired
  President, Board of Inquest, 14
berth deck companionway, 16
Bird, Homer, 99, 100, 101, 102, 103, 104, 105, 106, 111
Black and White Cold Cream, 94
Board of Inquest, 14, 15, 19
Bonnano, S.
  Quartermaster, 24
Bostwick
  Third Officer, Abarenda, 15
Bostwick, H.M.
  Third Officer, *Abarenda*, 24
Bremerton, Wash., 48
Brewer, L.
  Seaman, 24
Brewster
  Seaman, 10
brig, 9, 10, 11, 54, 94
British Navy, 19

British Registry, 112, 118
Brooklyn Daily Eagle, 19, 20, 23, 27
Brooklyn, New York, 19, 27, 47
Brutus, 7, 10, 23, 24, 25, 27, 63, 66
Bundick, 101
Bureau of Navigation, xii, 6, 7, 8, 13, 15, 24, 25, 50, 51, 52, 63, 64, 65, 119, 122
Bureau of Pensions, 1, 8, 61, 62, 63, 64, 65, 69, 72, 74, 79, 81, 82, 88, 89, 90
burial, 22, 96
Caesar
    collier, 10
Cahn, Bertrand, 71
Capias, 42, 47
Cardiff, England, 117
Carew, John Francis
    Congressman, NY, 79, 80, 81, 82, 84, 85, 86, 87
Casse, Marshall, 2, 3
Castorie, H.
    Seaman, 12
cause of death, 21, 22
Cavite, Philippines, 7
cemetery, 23, 96
Chief Officer, xii, 1, 7, 8, 14, 15, 16, 19, 20, 21, 52, 75, 96
Chinal, Louis E.
    Seaman, 10, 12, 44, 48, 49, 50, 51, 52, 53
code, 26

collier, vii, 6, 7, 9, 10, 11, 15, 22, 25, 42, 52, 53, 54, 57, 93, 112, 118, 119, 121
Collier Service, 6, 7, 120
Commissioner of Pensions, 1, 6, 58, 60, 64, 65, 68, 69, 71, 72, 74, 79, 80, 81, 82, 83, 84, 85, 88, 91
Commissioner V. Warner, 65
Companion-way, 12
Company D, 9th Infantry Regiment, 58
Coon, Irving, 89
Corporal Punishment, 43
court martial
    process not applicable, 15
Cowles, William C.
    Chief, Bureau of Equipment, USN, 26, 50
Cramer, 1
Croscup, Lucille Weichert, 93, 95
Daily Naval Report, 55
Davis, Robert C.
    Adjutant General, 85
De La Fonte, A.
    Fireman, 24
Denver Post, 23
Deserter, 11
deserters, 12, 14
Dickson, Alexander, 15, 17, 19, 32, 33, 40, 55
    Carpenter, 13, 15, 16, 17, 19, 20, 24, 25, 26, 31,

32, 33, 35, 40, 41, 52, 56, 75, 77
Disposition of Useless Papers, 123, 124
District Attorney, 15, 26
District Court, 13, 24, 28, 29, 31, 32, 41, 42, 43, 44, 45, 46, 47, 48, 49, 50, 51, 52, 53, 56, 104, 107, 108, 109, 110, 111
Dixon, A.
  Carpenter - incorrect name, 13
Dixon, George
  Carpenter - incorrect name, 13, 15
double irons, 9, 54, 55
Dr. McCarthy, 69
drunkenness, 10
Easton, William
  Seaman, 16, 24
Edwards Shipbuilding Company, Limited, 112, 113
El Caney, 59
eyewitness, 34
Fall
  Secretary of the Interior, 87
femoral artery, 18, 21
Fincke, W.
  Master, NAS, 27
First Officer, 7, 9, 14, 20, 23, 27, 54, 55, 64
Fobinatis
  Seaman, 9
Foley, T., 9
Fort Brooke Post Cemetery, 96
Fort San Juan, Cuba, 58, 59

Freudendorf, G, Chief
  Boatswain, U.S. Navy Recorder, Board of Inquest, 14
Fyskman, O.
  Boatswain, 24
Gadeberg, P.M.
  Second Officer, *Abarenda*, 24
Gaines, 99
Gallagher, Patrick
  Seaman, 10, 11, 12, 24, 45, 48, 49, 51, 52, 53
gallows, 111
Gardner, Washington
  Commissioner of Pensions, 83, 84
Gay, John L.
  Clerk, U.S. District Court for Porto Rico, 42, 50
gold, 100, 101, 104
Golden, Ruth Ann, 98
Goodro, John
  Boatswain, disrated to Seaman, 9, 13, 24, 48, 49
Graham Steamship Company, Limited, 112, 115
Grand Jury, 15, 25, 31, 42, 43
Griggs, John William
  U.S. Attorney General, 104
Guantanamo, Cuba, 119
Gustafsin, J.
  Quartermaster, 24
H. R. 18671, 63
H. R. 25613, 75, 76, 78

127

Halford, F., 1st Lieutenant, U.S.M.C.
  Member, Board of Inquest, 14
Hamill, James A.
  Congressman, NJ, 71, 74
Hampton-Roads, 25
Hartings, John, 2
Hastings, J. Walter, 3
Healy, 98
Healy, Andrew, 98
Healy, Catherine, 1, 2, 98
Healy, Mary, 1, 2, 4, 69, 95, 98, 99
Helena Mary Weichert, 4
Hell ship, 42
hemorrhage, 19, 22, 34
Holmes, J.W.
  Master, 119
homicide, 33, 37, 38, 40, 101
Hopkins, C.B.
  U.S. Marshal, 49
Howdon-on-Tyne, 112
Hurlin, Hans, 100, 101, 102, 103, 104
I have killed the mate, 16, 17
in the line of duty, 19, 60, 62, 76, 88
indictment, 31, 33, 35, 36, 37, 38, 39, 40, 43, 46, 49, 56, 75, 101
insolent and insulting language, 13
insubordination, 10, 12
irons, 9, 11, 16, 20, 25, 45, 46, 54, 55, 56, 57, 116

Jersey City, 1, 5, 23, 62, 65, 69, 72, 74, 77, 78, 93
jurisdiction, 31, 32, 35, 43, 44, 45, 46, 47
Kaiser, Marie, 1
Kelley, Anthony
  First Assistant engineer, *Abarenda*, 24
Kiefer, James
  U.S. Commissioner for the Western District of Washington, 49, 50
Kinkead, Eugene Francis
  Congressman, NJ, 75, 76, 77
Klee, 69, 90
Klee, Martha, 1, 69, 83
Klondike, 99, 100, 104
Knox, Attorney General, 105
Lamberts Point, 9, 119
Lathe, Fred M.
  Deputy U.S. Marshal, 49
Leake, Eugene, Walter
  Congressman, New Jersey, 63, 64, 65, 73, 77
Liverpool, 115, 117
Los Angeles Herald, 55
Love, Mary A., 69
Ludwig, Mary, 1, 2
Madrigal & Company of Manila, 122
Madrigal, Vicente, 122
Malone, James P., 2, 3
Maltreating Seamen, 43
manslaughter, 32, 33, 36, 37, 40, 52, 75

Marsden, George
　Seaman, 10, 11, 24, 45, 46, 48, 49, 51, 52, 53
　master, 10, 12, 43, 44, 45, 46, 47, 53, 54, 55
McDonald, George M., 7
McKinley, William Jr.
　President, 105
Metcalf, V. H.
　Navy Secretary, 25
military honors, 23
Miller
　Seaman, 11, 12
Minnesota
　battleship, 10, 56
Mixtae Religionis, 2, 3
murder, vii, 1, 8, 20, 21, 23, 24, 33, 36, 37, 55, 62, 63, 75, 104, 105
Naval Auxiliary Service
　N.A.S., 7, 15, 23, 54, 55, 57, 63, 119, 120
Navy Department, ix, xii, 6, 7, 13, 15, 21, 23, 25, 26, 63, 68, 72, 75, 76, 77, 78, 113, 119, 121, 123, 124
Navy Yard, ix, 9, 14, 15, 20, 21, 27, 47, 56, 118, 119, 122
Nelson, Knute
　Senator, Minnesota, 56
Nero
　collier, 10, 23, 24, 25, 27
New Orleans, ix, 1, 2, 3, 4, 6, 23, 60, 70, 72, 98, 99, 101, 111
New York Nautical College, 6
Newberry
　Acting Navy Secretary, 51

Newcastle on Tyne, 114, 115
newspapers, vii, 13, 22, 94
Nicholas, Thomas F., 83, 89
Nickels, E.D.P.
　Master, *Alexander*, 6
Norfolk, 7, 9, 14, 15, 25, 51, 52, 119
O'Donnell, Terrence J.
　United Spanish War Veterans, 89
offense, 10, 11, 54, 55
Official Report of Death, 21
orders, 10, 12, 14, 15, 48, 52
paint, 10, 13, 14
Paterno, S.R., 122
Patterson, 1, 2, 69, 70, 71, 95, 98, 99, 100, 101, 102, 103, 104
Patterson, Catherine, 99
Patterson, Ebenezer Angus, 98
Patterson, Jeff. D., 70
Patterson, Robert L., 1, 2, 71, 98, 99, 100, 104
Patterson, Viola, 3
Patterson, Viola Ruth, 1, 2, 70, 71
Pension, 1, 4, 5, 6, 7, 8, 21, 58, 60, 62, 63, 64, 65, 67, 68, 69, 70, 71, 72, 74, 75, 78, 79, 80, 81, 82, 83, 84, 85, 87, 88, 89, 90, 91, 92
Peperkorn, Hermann, 62
Pillsbury, John E., Rear Admiral, USN
　Chief, Bureau of Navigation, 50, 51, 52
Porto Rico, 28, 29, 31, 32, 33, 34, 40, 42, 46, 49
Porto Rico to *Puerto Rico*

Official change of
  spelling, 11
possemen, 106
Poupart's ligament, 18, 21
Prince, George W.
  Chairman Committee on
  Claims, House of
  Representatives, 76
prisoners, 10, 11, 55
Private Bill, 63, 75
Puerto Rico National
  Cemetery, 96, 97
punishment, 36, 43, 44, 45,
  46, 54, 55, 56, 57
Rampfeil, 95
Redgrave, De Witt Clinton
  Commander, USN, Ret.
  Asst. Supervisor, NAS,
  23
Regulations, 6, 7, 54, 55, 57,
  120
Rio de Janeiro, 9, 10, 11, 12,
  29
Robsion, John Marshall
  Congressman, KY, 87, 88,
  91
Rodey, Bernard Shandon,
  28, 31, 33, 34, 42
Rohrer, Karl
  Commandant, San Juan
  Naval Station, 15, 21
Roosevelt, Theodore
  President, 28, 29, 105
Saltzgaber
  Commissioner, Bureau of
  Pensions, 79, 81, 82
Samoa, 119, 121

San Juan Hill, 60
San Juan Military Cemetery,
  22, 96
San Juan Naval Station, xii,
  13, 15, 21, 24, 25, 26, 50,
  51, 52
San Juan, Porto Rico, 11, 13,
  23, 25, 35, 52
Santiago, Cuba, 60
Savage, José Ramon
  Fernandez, 29, 30, 31, 41,
  42, 48
Scheffler, Charles, 100, 101,
  102
Scotland, 117
Chinal, Louis E., 24
Second Officer, 7, 24, 63, 68
Shields, 115, 116
Shoemaker, W.R.
  Commander, USN, 1, 6,
  68
Shoup, James M.
  U.S. Marshal, 104, 105,
  106
Siboney, Cuba, 58
Sitka, Alaska, 105, 106, 111
Spanish American War, 58,
  119
St. Francis Orphan Asylum,
  93
St. John the Baptist Church,
  2, 3, 4
Stanley, H.A., USN
  Boatswain, 22
Strong, Norma, 99, 100, 101,
  102, 103

Supervisor of Naval
  Auxiliaries, 1, 23, 63, 64,
  68, 69
Sutton, J.W.
  Electrician, 24
telegraph, 26
The Daily Truth, 99
Third Officer, 6, 14, 24
threatening language toward
  first officer, 13, 56
Tieman, E. C.
  Acting Pensioner
  Commissioner, 80
Times-Picayune, 23
Titche, Bernard, 70, 71
trial, 24, 27, 32, 35, 37, 40,
  41, 47, 49, 50, 52, 55, 56,
  77, 101, 104, 115, 119
Tyzteman, Oscar
  Seaman, 13, 14
U.S. Army, 58, 60, 68
Todd, Elmer E., 48
U.S. Marshal, 23, 24, 25, 47,
  49, 50, 51, 52, 53, 104,
  105, 106
U.S.A.S., 7, 9, 14, 15, 19, 21
United Press, 20, 22
United Spanish War
  Veterans, 89, 90
United States Auxiliary Ship,
  9
United States Marshal, 47
USS *Concord*, 68
USS *Kearsarge*, 68
Van Names, John, 2
Vawter
  U.S. Deputy Marshal, 105,
  106
venereal disease, 12
Venezuela, 68

Veterans Administration, 1,
  22, 96
War Department, 61, 80, 85
Ward, 1, 93, 94
Warner, V.
  Commissioner, Bureau of
  Pensions, 69, 72
Webb, U.R.
  P.A. Surgeon, USN, 14,
  18, 19, 21
Wedding, 2
Weichert, Helena Mary, 4,
  95
Weichert, Joseph W., 1
Weichert, Robert Lawrence,
  4, 93
Weichert, Viola Ruth, 1, 4,
  23, 62, 63, 64, 65, 66, 67,
  68, 69, 70, 71, 72, 73, 74,
  75, 76, 77, 78, 79, 80, 81,
  82, 83, 84, 85, 86, 87, 88,
  89, 90, 91, 92, 93, 94, 98
  daughter, 4, 70, 74
Weichert, Walter Robert,
  viii, ix, xii, 1, 2, 3, 4, 5, 6,
  7, 8, 9, 14, 15, 16, 19, 20,
  21, 22, 23, 33, 35, 41, 54,
  58, 59, 60, 62, 63, 64, 65,
  66, 67, 68, 69, 70, 71, 72,
  74, 75, 76, 77, 78, 79, 80,
  81, 82, 83, 84, 85, 86, 87,
  88, 89, 90, 91, 92, 93, 94,
  96, 98
Western District of
  Washington, 29, 49, 50
Western Union Telegraphic
  Code, 26, 51
Winner, Mark H.
  Second Assistant
  Engineer, *Abarenda*, 24

Winthrop, Beekman
  Acting Navy Secretary, 76, 77
Worley, George W.
  Master, 7, 20, 21, 23, 25, 27, 41, 42, 43, 44, 45, 46, 47, 49, 50, 51, 52, 53, 56, 57, 63
Wounded in action, 60
wounds, 18, 19, 21, 34, 35, 36, 37, 47, 66, 73, 81, 104

www.ingramcontent.com/pod-product-compliance
Lightning Source LLC
Chambersburg PA
CBHW050816160426
43192CB00010B/1786